HOW TO

PROFIT FROM

JEWELLERY AND

ACCESSORIES

HOW TO PROFIT FROM JEWELLERY AND ACCESSORIES

ALISON JONES

ELMSBURY

First published in Great Britain in 2016 by Elmsbury Publishing UK

Parts of this book have been taken from How to Profit from Pet Products, by Alison Jones, Published November 2012 by Elmsbury.

10 9 8 7 6 5 4 3 2 1

A CIP catalogue record for this book is available from the British Library.

ISBN 978-0-9574878-2-6

Typeset in Liberation
Printed and bound in Great Britain

www.elmsbury.com

Contents

Preface

A few years after launching Prince & Princess Petwear, I decided to diversify into jewellery and accessories. It seemed the natural way forward, having sold the equivalent products for animals successfully for three years. It was also a great way to celebrate finishing the Business and Management degree that I had been reading for when I started Prince & Princess Petwear.

However, getting a foothold in the jewellery market proved much harder than the pet products market. I had planned to apply the same business model that I had used the first time around; testing the market with mid to low-end priced items on auction sites, while simultaneously building up a customer base, and eventually launching an ecommerce website. Not only was the jewellery and accessories market very different, but also in the three years since starting the pet accessories business, the retail landscape had changed somewhat.

Many of the categories on eBay were now saturated. Most significantly, in the jewellery categories, manufacturers from the Far East had joined the foray and had driven prices down so low it was almost impossible to make a profit through price or volume. It was clear that a different strategy was needed for the new business.

Through trial and error, an enthusiasm to learn about our new target market, and a willingness to try sales channels we hadn't considered before, Accessories Palace UK began to grow.

Taking that first step can be exciting and daunting in equal measure, but knowing where and how to get started is half the battle. I hope that *How to Profit from Jewellery and Accessories* will inspire both seasoned retailers andthose who are still just thinking about starting up, and help you on your way to building a successful and profitable business.

Alison Jones,
Founder, Accessories Palace

Acknowledgements

I am extremely grateful to all the jewellery and accessory retailers I consulted while researching this book. In particular, Debbie and Steven Shaw, and Jennifer, who shared their experiences, triumphs and failures with me.

I am forever indebted to the lecturers at St Helens College School of Business and Management, 2004-09. Without their knowledge, support and advice, www.accessoriespalace.co.uk, and this book, would not have been possible.

Finally, I would like to thank my editor at Elmsbury, for her invaluable guidance and hard work. Since I was able to incorporate some of the business concepts discussed in my first book, *How to Profit from Pet Products,* I hope you had less stress this time around!

# The Routes to a Jewellery & Accessories Business

There are many different ways to enter the jewellery and accessories market. You may be thinking about becoming, or already be, a specialist jewellery business, perhaps with a website or a bricks and mortar shop.

Service businesses that already operate in the industry, such as jewellery repairers, may wish to diversify into retail to generate an extra income and increase their customer base. Selling jewellery and accessories doesn't have to be confined to businesses already operating within the industry though. There are an increasing number of businesses, including gift shops, clothing boutiques and arts and craft centres, which have benefited from expanding into jewellery and accessories.

Whichever route you take, there are a number of factors that you should consider, which will help improve your chances of success.

The Specialist Jewellery & Accessories Business

The specialist focuses only on offering jewellery and accessories, which means that they can concentrate on retail without having to juggle an additional core activity, such as clothes retailing. To succeed, the specialist should consider the following:

Providing Something Different

There are countless companies out there that focus on offering just jewellery. It can be tempting for business owners to study these competitors with the aim of imitating them, especially when starting up with no previous experience of retail, or the jewellery industry. Instead of mimicking and becoming a clone, (and copying a rival's mistakes in the process,) specialists should look for ways to distinguish their business from the competition. There are numerous ways to do this, including by offering bespoke designs, an exclusive range of products, or a personal shopping service.

Become Even More Special

Because of the high level of competition in the industry, it helps if you can find a corner of the market that is (1) not currently being served by another company, (2) is growing, and (3) whose target customers have specific problems that you can solve. Some specialist shops are so niche they have become world-renowned, simply because they are the only outlet selling a particular product or range. A good example of this is Pandora, with its charm bracelet concept. Even though niche businesses serve a smaller number of customers than they would if they catered for everyone, customers are willing to pay a premium price for their specialist products.

To find your niche, you will need to think of a specific group of customers you can serve, such as brides of unusual themed weddings, plus-sized jewellery, or people looking to commemorate special occasions. It always helps if you have a passion for your chosen niche area. In fact, many small businesses are started by people who couldn't find what they were looking for as consumers.

Become an Expert

Customers expect jewellery and accessories retailers to be incredibly knowledgeable in a wide range of matters. They will ask what handbag will match their outfit, what earrings they should buy for sensitive skin, or which ring they should choose for their girlfriend.

Obviously, if you choose to build your business around a single innovative product, or focus on a particular style or occasion, then you won't need to have such an extensive knowledge. You will, however, still need to know your products in-depth.

Staying on Trend

One of the major difficulties jewellery and accessories businesses face is staying on-trend. Fashions come and go rapidly, so it is vital that you stay up-to-date. Customers simply won't return if they see that your shop is full of last season's items. In order to stay on-trend, you will need to know what styles are currently in vogue, and what is set to become popular in the future. To meet customer demand, you will need to be flexible, and you will need your suppliers to be flexible with a fast turnaround, too.

Quality is just as important as style, as far as customers are concerned. Thankfully though, having a wide choice of colours, sizes and finishes is less important.

Because retailers don't always get it right, and because trends can change overnight, having clearance sales to get rid of old stock, (often at break-even or a loss,) is something that jewellery and accessory retailers are all too familiar with. The pain of these quick sales will be exacerbated if you tend to buy products in all their possible colours and finishes. The likelihood is that it will be an entire style, rather than a particular colour, that doesn't sell, so any loss would be multiplied by the number of colour and size variations that you stock.

The Diversified Business

Existing businesses that start selling jewellery can generate an extra income, without having to find extra customers through expensive marketing. There are two types of diversification: lateral (jewellery related), and horizontal (non-jewellery related).

Jewellery-Related Diversification

Retailing jewellery and accessories can provide an extra income, and attract new customers to businesses that already offer a jewellery-related service, such as:

- Engraving
- Jewellery repairs and cleaning
- Goldsmiths and silversmiths
- Jewellery-making suppliers
- Bespoke designers
- Auctioneers and valuers
- Gemologists

To succeed, the jewellery-related diversifier should consider the following:

Capitalising on Trust

Professional businesses, such as watch repairers and valuers, need to be perceived as trustworthy in order to be successful. This presents a good opportunity to make additional income from retail, by capitalising on the confidence that customers already have in you. This is by no means taking advantage; you must meet pre-existing customer expectations by offering products that match the quality and value of the services that you already provide.

Impulse Buying

Low value impulse items placed strategically at the till point can increase the 'basket value' of each sale, and increase your revenue significantly.

It is much easier to get customers to add products to their bill at the point of sale. After all, they are about to pay for your services anyway, so in their minds an extra item or two is not going to make much difference.

Improve your Resource Efficiency

By diversifying, you can make better use of your existing resources and improve your efficiency. Perhaps there is an unused space on your premises that could be filled with a range of jewellery and accessory products. If you have a website that merely details the services you offer, you might feel that you could take advantage of the traffic visiting your site by transforming it into an ecommerce shop and generating revenue from it directly.

Non-Jewellery Related Diversification

It may be surprising, but you can sell jewellery and accessories in a wide variety of businesses, not just in the obvious outlets such as jewellery shops. This is good news if you are already running a business that seemingly has no association with the jewellery and accessories industry, including:

- Garden centres
- Department stores
- Gift and souvenir shops
- Arts and craft galleries
- Bridal shops
- Hairdressing and beauty salons

- Photography studios
- Charities

To diversify successfully, these businesses should consider the following:

Specialists Consider Existing Customers

Offering a huge range of jewellery and accessories is unlikely to be possible for all but the largest of non-jewellery related businesses, such as department stores. However, if you believe jewellery and fashion is important to your customers, you should try to find a way to develop your specialist range to include these products, whilst remaining loyal to the style, materials and area of expertise for which you are renowned. A leatherworker selling bags, purses, and jackets, could introduce a range of leather watches. A garden centre could look into garden-inspired jewellery and accessories. An equestrian business could consider stocking jewellery for horse lovers such as horseshoe necklaces and handbag charms, or perhaps equine-inspired bags and purses.

If there is a product range that will fit with your existing business, then you may be able to generate an extra income from it, but you must take into account your existing customer base. It is no good if your current customers are mostly conservative people and you introduce a line of punk rock style jewellery. This may be an obvious exaggeration, but you would be surprised just how many small businesses don't consider their existing customers when they are planning to diversify.

Provide the Expected

Diversifying into jewellery and accessories can give your business an edge, or at least make it an equal player if rivals already have market share in this area. In some businesses, a jewellery range is what customers now expect to see. When shopping in a clothing boutique for example, customers may expect to be able to buy an entire outfit, including the matching accessories. If a clothing shop offers just clothes, then shoppers may feel that there is something lacking from the store. Not only will the retailer miss out on the potential sales of jewellery and accessories, but also customers may find a more convenient competitor that offers clothes *and* accessories under one roof.

Seasonality

Selling jewellery and accessories can help businesses overcome seasonal lows; by reducing the impact that these quiet trading periods have on cash flow. Garden centres are a good example of this. Traditionally they struggled to get people through their doors during the winter months, but many have opened cafes, home ware and gift boutiques, and… jewellery and accessories departments. These additions have attracted new customers and kept their existing customers happy.

Another example can be found in bridal retailing. The low season in the UK wedding industry is November to April, and consequently bridal boutiques often struggle during the Christmas period. However, by diversifying into non-bridal jewellery and accessories, even if it is under a different brand name, wedding retailers can have a safety net during the quiet months.

Although the peak sales of jewellery and accessories are likely to occur in the run up to Christmas, turnover can be steady throughout the rest of the year because people will buy jewellery for everyday wear, and as gifts for birthdays and other occasions.

Use Products to Sell Them

If you can somehow incorporate the products that you sell into the delivery of your service, you may be able to generate further sales. For example, photography studios that offer makeover photo shoots could offer a few jewellery pieces for sale. Clients usually bring their own outfits and accessories, but there are always clients that forget to bring their own, or you may be able to persuade them to try on some of your pieces. Some studios, particularly those that specialise in vintage shoots, also sell the costumes, so it wouldn't be too much of a stretch to start selling jewellery. Since clients will be paying for the images anyway, it will be easier to sell to them.

Beware of the Risks

Diversifying into an area in which you have no prior experience can be risky. After all, you are putting your reputation, which you have built on some other product or service, on the line. You will need to attract new customers without discouraging your existing ones, so the decision to start retailing jewellery and accessories must be accepted by your target market.

Entering a new market is likely to take up more of your energy and may mean you have to acquire new skills and knowledge. It can be difficult to give sufficient time to a new venture if your primary business is demanding constant attention. The danger is that the challenges of diversifying may hamper your overall effectiveness and productivity, and this may damage the reputation of both your new and current areas of business. However, the decision to diversify is one that is often made when a business has reached a plateau in terms of revenue, and it needs to find new customers and markets to survive. In these cases, there is little or nothing to lose by trying something new. Even if there are no current problems, diversification can provide a safety net in case your sales start to drop in the other areas of your business.

In the next chapter, we will look at how to gather research on your target market, including the questions you will need to ask potential customers, in order to gain valuable information that you can use to design every part of your jewellery and accessories business.

Understanding the Market

B efore launching a new business or diversifying into jewellery, you will need to research the market.

Factors such as customers, competitors and the external environment can affect businesses in different ways, so it is vital that you conduct thorough research before you launch, and at regular intervals thereafter.

Despite its importance, some business owners believe that research is not necessary. They make the mistake of thinking that they can build a thriving business simply by imitating a successful competitor, or basing decisions upon assumptions such as "I like vintage style, therefore my customers will too." Many cite a lack of time as a reason for not doing enough research, so later on in this chapter we shall look at the ways to save time by incorporating marketing research into other activities.

The Two Types of Data

There are two types of data that you will need to collect: primary, and secondary.

Primary Data

Primary data is information that you gather firsthand from a group of people (your sample) that is representative of your target market.

The most popular primary data method used is the questionnaire, because you can obtain information from a large sample very cheaply, and it is relatively easy to analyse the data afterwards. If you decide to use this method, consider the length of your questionnaire carefully. Most people are busy and don't have the time or the inclination to be answering lots of questions. Therefore, you'll need to be selective about what you ask. Try to design a questionnaire that can be completed in less than five minutes.

Interviews are another popular method, as you can gain a lot of in-depth information from individuals, either over the phone or face to face. However, due to the time it takes to recruit and interview enough people, this method is usually only used when there is a lot of money at stake, such as when researching and developing a new mass-market product.

A focus group is made up of a small number of people that meet to have an in-depth discussion about a particular topic, such as the latest style trends. It usually takes a lot of preparation and a highly skilled researcher to steer a focus group without influencing the participants' responses. An informal brainstorming session with friends or customers may be just as productive, and certainly cheaper to implement, providing the members of the group can contribute constructively. Friends and family will nearly always tell you that your ideas are wonderful, so take what they say with a pinch of salt until you can confirm your findings with further research.

Another method is mystery shopping, which is a legitimate way to gather data on a competitor. If a rival has no internet presence, then visiting their shop or telephoning may be the only way to discover information about them. By posing as a genuine customer, you can find out a lot, including how they treat customers, the prices they charge, the level of competence of the staff, and the overall shopping experience they provide.

There is much to be learned from your dealings with any business, not just your competitors in the jewellery and accessories industry. Always be in research mode whenever you are a customer yourself, as the ideas that you are exposed to may be useful in creating a competitive edge, and a better shopping experience for your own customers.

Secondary Data

Secondary data is information that has been produced or collected by someone else. Secondary sources include:

- Magazine and newspaper articles
- Websites, blogs and forums
- Government statistics
- Research reports
- Company documents
- Brochures, flyers and leaflets
- News and documentaries
- Trade associations or business advisory services
- Social media and business network sites
- Customer reviews

When it comes to secondary data, you'll need to decide whether your sources are reliable. An article published in an academic journal is probably more reliable than a news story printed in a tabloid newspaper, even if it was published more recently.

Collecting Your Data

It is best to collect secondary data first as it will give you an indication of the topics you need to focus on for the primary research, as well as the best methods of collecting this information.

There are three main areas of research you should cover; your potential customers; your competitors; and external factors.

Your Potential Customers

The aim of analysing your prospective customers is to identify the markets that you should be targeting, and to find out their needs and wants so that your company can fulfil them.

Basic Information – What is their age, gender, job, income, location, marital status, lifestyle and hobbies?

Shopping Habits – Where do they buy jewellery and accessories (e.g., online, high street, supermarket)? Which shops do they currently buy from? How much and how often do they spend on jewellery? How often do they purchase particular items of jewellery and accessories? What is their minimum and maximum spend for these products? What features do they look for (e.g., colour, brand name, style, price)? Are they spending more, the same or less on jewellery than they were a year ago? How far are they are willing to travel to buy fashion accessories? Who are they buying for? How many times do they visit a shop before they purchase low, mid, and high priced items?

Attitudes and Opinions – What do people think about aspects of your existing or proposed business (such as your pricing, branding, and product range)? What are their attitudes towards existing products on the market? What are their favourite and least favourite jewellery and accessory brands, and why? Which brands, if any, do they follow on social networking sites and why (e.g., for style tips, offers, discount codes, fashion news)?

Issues and Challenges – What problems have they encountered when shopping for jewellery for themselves or others, and how could your business solve these problems? Have they bought items from abroad because they are unavailable or too expensive in the UK? What good and bad experiences have they had while shopping for fashion accessories? What suggestions do they have for your products, services, pricing... etc?

Your Competitors

The aim of analysing your competitors is to discover their strengths and weaknesses, to find out what makes them successful, and ultimately to identify any gaps in the market.

Identify competitors – How many players are in the market? How many businesses will be in direct competition with you (because they have the same business as you), and who will be in indirect competition with you (because they run a similar business)? How much do they dominate? Are there any opportunities to take some of their market share?

History & Operations – How long they have been trading? How many staff do they employ? What are their hours of operation? Have they recently moved into bigger premises or diversified into new markets, or do they appear to be downsizing? What is the size of their operation (do they have a warehouse or are they a home-based business)? What are their policies (do they offer free delivery or an extended returns period)? What pricing strategies and sales channels do they use? What are their plans for the future?

Products – How extensive is their product range? Will they be competing with you directly? Do their products and services address specific problems that their customers have? Are their products innovative? Which brands do they stock? Do they have any exclusive licensing agreements? What products and services do they offer that you don't or can't provide?

Revenue – The revenue of a non-incorporated competitor is usually extremely difficult to find out. However, for a nominal fee you can download the accounts and documents of limited companies from www.companieshouse.gov.uk. This information can provide a benchmark for your own revenue targets.

Marketing – What media do your competitors use to promote themselves (e.g., a website, magazines, social media)? How do they use social networking sites (e.g., do they offer discount codes, engage with customers, promote new products)? How regularly do they advertise or promote themselves? Are they using Pay Per Click advertising? Which group(s) of people do they appear to be targeting? What is their branding like and is it consistent? Do they capture customer details by offering a newsletter or other incentive? What is their apparent marketing budget?

Service - How well do they build relationships with customers over the phone, by email, or in person? Do they ask customers the right questions? How do they encourage people to buy? Are they knowledge-able about the products that they are selling? What after-sales care do they offer? Do they offer loyalty schemes or other incentives?

Customers – What do customers love and dislike about your competitors? Why do they keep buying from them or why did they stop? What have people written about the service, products and other aspects of their business on review sites and online forums?

The External Environment

The aim of examining the external environment is to identify any factors that could impact how your business operates. This part of your research will highlight the costs imposed upon your business, and whether there will be continued consumer demand.

Economic – How does an economic downturn affect the buying behaviour of jewellery buyers (do they reduce their spending by buying accessories with a lower ticket price or by buying less frequently)? How do improvements in the economy affect buying behaviour (does the number of people buying jewellery increase, does spending increase)? How will exchange rates, taxation, interest rates, and import legislation have an impact on your business?

Social – How are the demographic factors of the population changing? Are households with children increasing (and do parents therefore have less to spend on non-essential items such as jewellery and accessories)? What current buying trends exist amongst jewellery and accessories customers? What attitudes exist towards buying fair trade, handmade, British-made, mass-made and foreign-made jewellery? How do topical debates, such as the impact of our throwaway society, affect buying behaviour? Which celebrities influence sales of jewellery and accessories? What fashion blogs and social networking sites are most popular? Could your business capitalise on big events such as Valentine's Day, a Royal Wedding, or The World Cup by selling themed items?

Technological – How will advances in technology change the way you communicate with, and market to, your customers in the future? How often will your website become outdated (due to new design trends, updates in payment technology, and screen-resolution changes?) Will the increase in smartphones change how your customers buy from you in the future? Will you be able to afford to keep up to date with technological advances? Will you still be able to compete if you cannot afford to adopt new technologies?

Political – How will taxation, trading and employment laws affect the way you operate your business? What new laws and directives are due to come into force in the near future? How would hypothetical (worse case scenario) changes to legislation, such as stricter lead content regulations, impact your business? Are there any government grants available to you? Are there any 'buy local' initiatives in your area and what positive or negative impact will these have on your business?

Environmental – How will the growing concerns about the environment affect your business decisions? What new markets have been created due to the public's raised awareness of climate change? Could the weather and climate change have an effect your sales, product ranges and insurance premiums?

Legal – How will the Sale of Goods Act (1979) affect your policies and the way that you source products? How will advertising laws affect your marketing? Will employment laws such as the Working Time Directive and the Health and Safety at Work Act (1974) increase your costs? Do you need to incorporate the Consumer Protection (Amendment) Regulations (2014) in your terms and conditions? What other laws are relevant to your business?

Analysing & Making Conclusions

Once you have collected your data, you will need to analyse your findings. Presenting the data in pie charts and graphs can make it easier to identify patterns and form conclusions. Not all data will lend itself to being shown in a chart though. The responses to some open questions can be long and varied, and therefore very difficult to collate visually.

By making inferences and drawing conclusions you can decide how best to proceed with each of the elements that make up your business (such as branding, pricing, and product range), and most importantly, whether it will be a viable venture.

Figure 2.1 gives examples of some possible conclusions you could make about your research findings. Research analysis is largely an exercise in common sense, but there may be times when it is not obvious what you should deduce and you'll need to conduct further research. If you had a large number of contemporary jewellery fans in your sample, then it would be right to conclude that your business needs to focus on contemporary jewellery, but what conclusion would you make about someone who travels ten miles to a jewellery & accessories boutique, when there is a jewellery shop two streets away? Perhaps their preferred boutique's opening times are more convenient, it could be the nearest stockist of their favourite brand, or maybe the customer is simply not aware that the local shop exists. Sometimes there are many possible explanations for a single finding, but if you have permission from your sample to contact them again in case you need further clarification, you can avoid jumping to the wrong conclusions.

Ongoing Market Research

People tend to be good at conducting market research before starting their business or diversifying. Once launched, owners are often far too busy with the day-to-day running of the business to find time to update their original research. In addition, some owners fail to realise just how rapidly customers, competitors, trends and other external factors can change.

Fortunately, ongoing market research doesn't have to be a massive drain on your time and resources, as it is something that can be easily incorporated into other business activities, to help you stay one step ahead and meet changing customer needs.

Monitoring Customers

Every interaction with customers is an opportunity to conduct research, and check that your original findings are up to date. You can gain valuable marketing information by dropping the odd research question into a friendly conversation, or inviting customers to make use of a suggestion box. When you actively solicit opinions in this way, you show your customers that they are important to you, which will help you engender loyalty.

Figure 2.1 Examples of Findings and Possible Conclusions

Finding	Possible Conclusion
There are several jewellery boutiques in town.	You will need to be sure that you can offer a better service, and that customers are willing to try a new shop.
Your sample buys only real-leather handbags that are of a high quality and good design.	Your branding and products need to reflect these values in order to appeal to these customers.
Members of your sample have high-powered jobs and often go for after-work drinks.	Customers will need conservative jewellery and accessories for work, and evening jewellery. You could consider reversible and interchangeable products.
Some members of your sample have regular nights out.	Customers will be looking for evening jewellery and accessories.
The government is planning to increase the minimum wage.	You may have to sell more products, increase prices, or cut costs (e.g., staff.)
The majority of people in your sample have children.	You could focus on offering a children's range, or bespoke commemorative jewellery if these niches will be lucrative.
The sample buys both high- and low-end products.	Are there specific products that customers demand at either a high or a low price? You may have to offer some products in a choice of price points, (e.g., the same ring in different metals.)
There is a local campaign to encourage people to buy fair trade or eco-friendly products.	If you think the campaign will strike a chord with consumers you should stock fair trade products or publicise how eco-friendly your business is.

If you use social networking sites such as Twitter and Facebook to promote your business, you can also use them to pose research questions. You could get your followers to vote for possible new products, or ask if a particular style is still in fashion, for example.

Instead of giving away discounts and other incentives, why not make customers earn some of their rewards by getting them to participate in market research? A completed questionnaire in exchange for 5% off, for example, will benefit both you and your customers.

If you collect the same data repeatedly (such as customer satisfaction surveys,) then try to automate this if possible to save yourself time. An online shop must send a confirmation email to the customer when their order has been dispatched. A link could be included in the email inviting recipients to answer a brief after-sales survey, which could be set up using a questionnaire software service such as Surveymonkey.com. All that would be left to do is for the online shop owners to check their performance regularly.

Monitoring Competitors

Monitoring your competitors can be less time-consuming if you take an organised approach and create a matrix, (see Figure 2.2.) With a matrix, you can monitor any other aspects of rival businesses that you think might be useful. You might decide to add rows that examine their pricing policies, customer service, corporate identity, marketing and promotions. A final row, 'Action', can be used to identify the gaps that your competitors have left, and the course of action that your own business should take to improve its competitive position.

You may have a list of twenty or thirty competitors depending on your business's circumstances, but you only need to examine a few of these each week in order to stay up-to-date. Because you will only be looking for *changes* that your competitors have made, rather than collecting the information from scratch, you will only need to set aside a short amount of time.

Online retailers are easy to monitor, but if some of your rivals are pure bricks and mortar businesses, you'll need to check up on them in person.

Figure 2.2 Example of a Competitor Analysis Matrix

	Competitor A	**Competitor B**
Products	Range of jewellery and accessories for all ages, occasions and styles.	Bridal jewellery, large selection of tiaras.
Channels	Online	Shop, online and events
Strengths	Offers customers a choice of delivery options, free returns, and a guarantee. Website is professional and on-trend.	Has been trading for fifteen years. Launches new promotions regularly. Has brand exclusivity.
Weaknesses	Doesn't have a wide men's jewellery range (although this is growing). Handbags and hair accessories seem to be aimed at the 35 to 45 age range only.	Not very well known outside of the town, has a dated website, and unfavourable customer policies.
Action	Look into the viability of men's jewellery, and accessories for younger ages. Review delivery options and customer policies.	Try to gain exclusivity of a brand, launch more promotions, and possibly advertise outside of the town.

To save time, try to do this while you are out doing your own shopping. If you attend shows or other events, aim to set up early so you have time to check out the competition before the doors open to the public.

As well as updating your matrix, you should also keep an eye out for new competitors entering the market. Do a regular quick Google search for jewellery and accessories in your area, and see if you recognise any new players. As discussed in Chapter 1, there are many different types of business that could start selling jewellery and accessories, and thus, potential competitors could appear anywhere. You'll save yourself time and avoid unpleasant surprises by paying attention to what is happening around you.

Monitoring the External Environment

It is always wise when running a business to look out for to any local, national, and international news stories about external factors. A quick scan of the news pages on the internet, or a listen to the business news on the radio on the way to work, can alert you to any forthcoming issues and give you time to plan ahead. Trade publications, such as Attire Magazine, are valuable too because they cover national business news stories, but discuss the effects that the issues have specifically on the jewellery and fashion industry.

Another way to monitor the external environment is by attending business and networking events. These events are more than just an opportunity to raise awareness of your business. As an attendee you will get to learn a lot about what is happening in your locality. When you are one of the first to hear about a new local government initiative, or a chain store moving into a nearby retail park, you'll have more time to prepare, and you'll have an edge over any competitors that don't network.

In the next chapter, we will look at the best sales channels you can use to reach your target market, together with the set-up and running costs, customer expectations and profitability.

Choosing the Right Sales Channels

Choosing the right sales outlets is about deciding the best way to deliver products and marketing information to your target market. Thanks to the advent of the internet, and most recently smartphones, businesses now have more sales channels to choose from than ever before:

- Retail premises
- Online shop
- Mobile commerce
- E-marketplaces
- Mail order
- Telemarketing
- Events
- Direct sales

The sales channels you choose are an important factor in your ability to make a profit. While you may harbour dreams of running a bricks and mortar shop, or of being an internet entrepreneur, if these channels don't meet the needs of your target market or your business, then success will be difficult.

Multi-Channel Retailing

M ulti-channel retailing, or selling through more than one channel, is an effective strategy for jewellery and accessories retailers. It is a way to develop the customer shopping experience and increase revenue and growth.

You are more likely to reach a broad range of customers if you are operating more than one channel, not least because prospective customers tend to be reassured by businesses that have expanded into two or more channels.

Multi-channel retailing can improve the efficiency of an operation through better sharing of its resources. For example, if you buy a van to run a direct sales channel, you can also use it to attend shows and events, and thus generate maximal revenue from the van. You'll also benefit from economies of scale, whereby the more sales you generate across the channels, the cheaper it becomes to make those sales, because you'll be using your equipment and time more efficiently.

Another benefit, which becomes apparent when one sales channel starts under-performing, is that you have the other channels to fall back on. This may also mean that you have an advantage over rivals that rely on just one channel, particularly if a problem becomes industry- or retail-wide. Imagine that your only outlet is a website, and that that website suffers a technical issue, which results in it being down for a few days. For those few days you are missing out on your only source of income. If, however, you happen to also sell on eBay and through home parties, you can still generate revenue while the website problem is being fixed. Therefore, any problems that you may encounter in one channel will have less of an impact on your business if you operate other channels.

Having more than one channel enables you to set different prices for your products based on each channel's target audience, location, and overheads. This strategy can cause a few headaches though. You may find yourself on the receiving end of complaints and bad reviews if customers discover that a product they bought via your website would have been cheaper in your shop. Honesty and transparency is key, as we discuss later in Chapter 6.

Customers increasingly expect to have an integrated shopping and brand experience. If a customer buys an item on your website, they expect to be able to return it to your store. Similarly, shoppers like to know that if they spot a necklace on your market stall, they can order it later from your web or mobile-optimised site.

With a multi-channel strategy, stock control, bookkeeping and other administrative tasks could become more complex and time-consuming. Ideally, you should integrate these systems into a single system that all of your channels share. Multi-channel systems, whether they are off the shelf or bespoke, can be expensive, but they will help you to achieve consistency across your brand.

Choosing The Right Channels

Whether you choose to sell jewellery and accessories through one channel or several, you need to ensure that the channel(s) you choose are going to:

- **Reach your target market** – Will you be able to reach enough potential customers through the channel? Which channels do your existing and potential customers prefer?

- **Be cost effective** – What are the costs and how quickly can you recuperate these costs? Some channels are inexpensive to set up, while some require time and a lot of hard work before you can break-even. You need to be certain that a new channel can generate enough extra income to make it worthwhile. If you were to start selling online for example, you'd need to take into account the initial outlay of designing and launching a website, as well as the ongoing costs such as search engine optimisation and site maintenance.

- **Offer customers an integrated brand experience** – Can customers that buy products from your online shop then return them to your physical shop if they need to? Are you able to offer the same or a larger product range across your channels? Delivering an integrated brand experience can be a challenge if you are on a budget, as it means that all of your systems, particularly your Electronic Point of Sale (EpoS), need to be in-built to work centrally.

- **Match your business values and vision** – If your business is all about being eco-friendly, then launching a gas-guzzling sales van is hardly supporting your core values. If your business is keen to provide a personal one-to-one service, you are more likely to achieve this with premises, events, and direct selling, rather than with ecommerce or mobile commerce. Think about what is important to your customers and choose your channels accordingly.

Over the following subchapters, we'll look in-depth at the most appropriate channels for selling jewellery and accessories, what expectations customers have, the level of competition you'll face, and whether you'll generate a good profit.

Sales Channels: Retail Premises

Having a shop can be a highly rewarding and lucrative way to sell jewellery and accessories. It can be hard work and involve long hours, but it offers social interaction with customers as well as the chance to become a part of your local community.

Understandably, the almost daily reports about the state of the High Street discourage people from opening new shops. For every business closure though, there are many more stories of businesses having success, even those trading in the shadow of large competitors such as Claire's Accessories, Accessorize and H. Samuel.

A major plus to running a shop, is that customers tend to perceive a business with physical premises as being more trustworthy than those operating via some of the other channels.

Customer Expectations

When shopping in a small independent store, customers expect a personal experience provided by friendly staff. Most people like to be acknowledged when they enter, and encouraged to approach staff for help if they need it. Your staff need to be knowledgeable in the benefits and features of every product, and be able to offer advice to customers when they are buying for specific occasions.

The interior of your shop should be inviting, clean and uncluttered. The people visiting your store will expect to be able to find what they are looking for quickly and easily, so a good layout with clear signage and accessible shelving is essential. Offering a wide range is usually preferable. However, while you want your shop to look full and complete, you don't want it to be overcrowded with too many products. Cramming every surface, shelf, and wall with stock can make a place look cluttered and disorganised, and customers won't be able to see any of your products properly.

Many customers hate having to ask the price of items, so transparent pricing on all of your products is a must. The only exception to this is if you are serving an extremely high-end clientele that doesn't care how much they spend.

Many of the large jewellery and accessories retailers now offer a Click and Collect option, which is usually easy to set up on most ecommerce sites. A local delivery service is something that you could consider, too.

Finally, your shop should be more than just a shop. In the current climate, there is an increasing demand for retailers to create 'social hubs', by arranging events and activities for customers. A coffee morning or a jewellery making class will give people a reason to visit the high street and your store, while exclusive VIP events are a way to reward customer loyalty.

Costs

There are normally greater overheads associated with having premises compared to the other sales channels. These include:

Premises

Finding the right premises can be a long process, which usually ends in a trade-off between rent (or mortgage) and factors such as location, accessibility and floor space. If you plan to rent premises, then you'll need to put down a deposit (typically up to six months' rent in advance.) Furthermore, landlords will often try to tie you into a lengthy lease agreement, so be prepared and always try to negotiate down.

Business Rates and Stamp Duty

Business rates are a tax imposed by local authorities on the occupiers of commercial property, and are based on a valuation of the premises. This tax may be included in the rent, but you will definitely need to pay stamp duty, which is payable on all commercial leases.

Utilities, Maintenance and Repair

An ongoing cost associated with having a shop is utilities, such as water and electricity. If you own, rather than rent, a business property, then you are also responsible for its maintenance, repairs, building and contents insurance, and anything else that a landlord would normally take care of. Don't forget that if your business needs information services (i.e. broadband internet) this will be an additional ongoing cost, unless you're lucky enough to find a property where the internet is already provided. Sometimes repairs and utilities are included in a service charge, but make sure that you are clear about what is covered before you sign the lease.

Fixtures, Fittings and Signage

To keep customers in your shop for as long as possible, the interior must be appealing and inviting. Good display fittings can be expensive, so check with your suppliers to find out if they provide Point of Sale units with their products, as this could reduce your costs quite considerably. Lighting is essential, not only for safety, but also to show off your products in the best possible way. Professional signage is an important part of your branding, and if you have a large shop floor, interior signs can help customers find what they are looking for more easily.

Stock

The amount of stock you need depends on the floor space of your shop and the type of display units you have. Obviously, the more stock you buy the more sales it will require to break-even. To reduce your stock expenditure, you could try to persuade a supplier to offer their goods on a sale or return basis.

Legal

If you have customers visiting your premises then public liability insurance is a legal requirement. Product liability may be worth considering if it is not included in the policy. Jewellery and accessories retailers, especially those stocking fine jewellery, are a common target for break-ins, and this may be reflected in your premiums (even if you have the world's best security system in place.) If you employ staff, you must get employers' liability insurance, which is required by law under the Employers' Liability (Compulsory Insurance) Act (1969).

Advertising

If you are a newly launched business, you will probably need to spend significant amount of money on advertising to get customers through your doors. Existing businesses that are diversifying into retail can usually take advantage of the mailing list they've already built up, and promote directly to existing customers to keep costs down.

Competition

The competition from larger high street chains, supermarkets, and the huge number of online businesses can cause the independent shop owner many a sleepless night. However, if you can focus on the things that your larger competitors find difficult to do, such as offering a personal shopping experience, bringing out the latest styles quickly, and exceptional customer service, then you will be well on your way to gaining a competitive advantage.

Competitor research is vital. In some areas, the market may be so saturated with jewellery and accessories shops that adding your own business would not be viable. Even if you have the monopoly in your town, you may still face indirect competition from online boutiques, due to people making price comparisons via their devices. However, if you have your own range or an exclusive brand, you can avoid the problem of having customers looking for cheaper alternatives.

Profitability

The location of your premises plays a massive part in your profitability. Your shop obviously needs to be wherever your target market is. Other factors, such as passing trade, customer parking, public transport links, and the reputation of the area, need to be sufficient before you can earn back your initial and ongoing costs, and start generating a steady income.

Having retail premises is one of the most expensive channels for a business to run, so keeping tight control of your outgoings is essential. It may be a good idea to offer a service alongside retailing jewellery and accessories, to achieve better cost and resource efficiency.

Studies have shown that customers feel more confident buying from a shop than through some of the other channels, especially ecommerce, where buyers have to trust that the seller will deliver and the products will match their descriptions. Possibly the biggest advantage of having shop premises is that customers are able to touch and feel products before they buy. For many, checking the quality, size, and colour of an item personally is a prerequisite to making a purchase. Shop owners must therefore strike the right balance between product accessibility for the customer (which increases sales) and product security (which reduces the cost of damage and theft). If your products need to be protected in glass cases, then it is vital to have approachable and attentive staff who will show the products to customers.

Another reason customers may trust a shop more is because it appears to be permanent and stable. When a customer knows there is a physical location they can return to if they have a problem, they are more likely to buy. However, in order for customers to feel confident about buying, they must feel that staff are friendly, professional and capable of dealing with issues.

Sales Channels: Online

Without a doubt, the internet has transformed the way we buy and sell. No longer are business owners required to 'man the till' to make sales. With ecommerce, your website is a shop that has neither geographical boundaries nor closing times.

The adoption of internet shopping has made it easier for existing businesses to expand and reach a global audience, while taking advantage of having few extra overheads. Even stay-at-home mums and those with full-time jobs have been able to benefit by launching their own online businesses from their spare rooms. However, this increased accessibility has resulted in fierce competition within the industry.

Companies entering this sales channel must be able to keep pace with the ever-changing technology and the needs of customers. There are however, a number of low-cost and even free ways to implement this channel, as will be discussed.

Customer Expectations

People who shop for jewellery and accessories online want to be able to find what they are looking for quickly and easily, so a good search facility is essential.

Customers aren't merely looking for products though; they are seeking information and style advice to assist them in the buying process. A credible online shop that knows everything there is to know about jewellery, accessories, and the latest fashion trends, is bound to be a hit with buyers.

Online customers expect a smooth and secure shopping process with clear pricing and delivery charges. They also expect to be given an estimated delivery time and to receive their goods swiftly, sometimes within 24 hours of placing an order. Offering favourable policies such as free returns, helps to reassure customers and reduce any pre-purchase anxiety they have when ordering online.

For customers, the major downside to shopping for accessories online is not being able to touch and feel the products before they buy. Therefore, high quality images that can be enlarged or have a zoom-in function, customer photos, and video demonstrations, can all help reduce the uncertainty that a customer may feel before buying. They can also make the experience of shopping on the website a lot more interesting.

Live Chat is becoming essential for web stores because many customers are looking for instant answers to their queries. It makes sense to try to answer their questions while they are still browsing and are presumably ready to buy. Equally, links to social networking sites such as Twitter, Google+, and Facebook are almost obligatory too, not least because customers like to ask their friends what they think of a product before they buy.

Costs

There are a number of fixed and ongoing costs associated with this sales channel, and it is important that you investigate them all fully before going ahead.

Functionality

Whether you plan to hire a designer, sign up to an ecommerce solution, or build a website yourself, you need to ensure that your website will meet both your requirements and those of your customers. You should begin by creating a list of website functions that you think will be essential, as well as functions that would be beneficial but are not crucial to your operation or competitiveness. Cost may limit what you eventually end up with, but this way you'll know the minimum you'll have to pay to get a website that works for your business.

Shopping functionality - Some shopping functions you may want to offer:

- Multiple currency and language options
- Discount and loyalty schemes
- Personalised products
- Recommendation engine
- Search engine
- Product variant selector for different colours and sizes
- Product image zoom-in or pop-up
- Customer accounts and order tracking
- A user experience without adverts, banners and pop-ups
- Live Chat
- Gift wrapping option

Back-office functionality - The back end is where everything happens for the online shop owner. Undoubtedly, its key function is to show all the orders that have been received, along with their status (paid, packed, dispatched, or returned, etc.) Sophisticated websites will perform more functions than just this though. It's wise to think ahead about the features you'll need because they will make life much easier, and in many cases, help you provide better customer service.

Possible functions could include:

- Automated order and dispatch confirmation emails
- Integration with software, e.g., EPoS and bookkeeping
- Integration with e-marketplaces
- Ability to manage your website from a device
- Payment gateway integration
- Social media integration
- Own domain name
- Ability to generate branded invoices and other documents
- Integration with fulfilment house and shipping carriers
- Stock control
- Availability of statistical data, e.g., sales reports
- Ability to import CSV files from a drop-shipper

Design and Creation

Once you have a clear idea of what you want, you can look for the best solution. There are a number of options available, you could:

Build a website from scratch - Of all the ways to get online, having a new website designed and built is generally the most expensive, (unless you have the skills and experience to do it yourself.) Complex projects can take months to be completed, but the result should be a unique website that looks exactly as you want it to, and has all the features that your business requires.

Sign up to a fully hosted ecommerce platform - There are numerous ecommerce platforms available, which, for a monthly or annual fee, provide a ready-made solution for retailers looking to sell their jewellery and accessories online. Shopping carts, such as Jimdo, EKM, Shopify and Lemonstand, offer various price plans and different features. Many offer free trials, which are great opportunities to see just how user friendly they are before making a commitment to one of them.

Download an open source ecommerce platform - Free, open source platforms such as Magento, Zen Cart, OS Commerce, and Presta Shop, require hosting as well as a database file manager such as FileZilla. You will need to have some HTML and CSS coding knowledge if you want to customise your website yourself. There are templates that you can buy or download free, which should reduce the amount of web designing you'll need to do. Alternatively, you could hire a web developer from a services marketplace such as Fiverr.com, or find a remote assistant from a provider such as Upwork.com, to keep your costs down.

Get a free website and add a payment facility - You could sign up for a basic informational website with Wordpress or Blogger and then add PayPal payment buttons or Wordpress's own plugin, to transform it into an online shop. By far the best free ecommerce option currently available though is Weebly. It is fully hosted, has customisable templates and you can use your own domain. Moreover, it provides a choice of payment options including PayPal.

If you plan to use Facebook, you can download an 'F-commerce' app, which will allow you to set up either a standalone store on your Facebook fan page, or integrate a Facebook shop front with your ecommerce site.

Domain & Hosting

It doesn't cost much to register a domain name with a provider such as Go Daddy. You should try to choose a web address that is easy to remember. The best domain names tell your customers what you do, and even state your location if you have a geographical territory, such as 'bristoljewelleryboutique.com'.

It is advisable to get both the dot co.uk and dot com in case people type the wrong URL, and to prevent someone from buying the domain and then forwarding your traffic to their own site. Ideally, your web address should be easy to spell, but if you think there is a chance your URL will be misspelled it may be worth buying those addresses too.

If your website is not already hosted, then you will also need to pay for hosting for your site's files, which usually costs a nominal amount each month.

Increasing your Website's Visibility and Traffic

The weeks and months following the launch of your website may demand your biggest advertising expenditure, as you push to increase traffic and break-even. Pay Per Click Advertising is the most popular method. However, once your website starts to show up naturally in the SERPs (Search Engine Results Pages,) you can reduce this amount considerably.

In order for the pages of your website to show up on the likes of Google and Yahoo, it needs to be optimised (more on this in chapter 7). Search engine optimisation is not a one-off process. As trends change, you'll have to modify the keywords you are targeting in order to maintain your page rankings. Search engines also like to see fresh content such as new blog entries, to prove that the site is still active. If this is not something you plan to do yourself, then you can hire a firm to do the job for you.

Another way to increase online traffic is by placing adverts on other websites. For these ads, you either pay a one-off fee, or ideally pay for the results that they yield, such as click-throughs or sales.

Payment Acceptance

Payment gateways, such as Sage Pay and PayPal, process your customer's credit or debit card details, take payment, and then transfer the payment into your bank account. For this service, providers may charge a transaction fee or a percentage fee of the sale, or both. Sometimes, this is in addition to an annual fee. The merchant accounts with the lowest fees may not necessarily be the most suitable for your business, so do some research. Ultimately, the best account is with a merchant that your customers trust.

Offline payment methods such as cheques, cash on delivery and direct bank transfers may not be as popular as they once were, but some customers prefer them, and usually you don't incur a fee if this is how customers choose to pay you.

Competition

Competition can be fierce, so online jewellery and accessories shops need to avoid competing on price and instead focus on gaining a competitive advantage in other ways, such as by building a strong brand, sourcing unique and exciting products, offering great customer service, and providing an amazing online shopping experience.

Your website should match, if not exceed, the standard set by your competitors if you are to have any chance of getting a foothold in the online jewellery and accessories market. An online shop needs to look visually appealing and professional, and be easy to navigate.

Large online retailers have much bigger budgets for web development and site upgrades, advertising, and product development. Therefore, you will need to find smart ways to keep up with them.

Profitability

An online shop is the perfect partner to all the other sales channels, but it can be a highly profitable channel in its own right.

The biggest hurdle to overcome is getting customers to trust your website and payment security. Appearance plays a big part in this, so you'll probably need to invest a lot upfront in order to get a professional-looking website, which appears trustworthy to visitors. Generally, the initial and ongoing costs are small in relation to the potential return you can make from reaching the huge worldwide audience on the web. In fact, compared to some of the other sales channels, ecommerce can be one of the cheapest to launch and operate, particularly if you run it from home or existing business premises.

Favourable policies always encourage customers when purchasing from an online business for the first time. However, anything that slows down the checkout process, such as an extensive list of delivery options, can give customers time to change their minds and could reduce your revenue. There is a fine line between offering convenience and offering unnecessary choices. The latter comes from not knowing who your customers are and what your customers want.

Finally, a recommendation engine will facilitate cross-selling, if you have a number of different groups of related products. You can relate products by design, style, occasion, size, colour, brand, and materials. By showing customers the matching products that will complete their look, you can significantly increase your online revenue.

Sales Channels: Mobile

M-commerce is the newest addition to the range of sales channels, and is currently growing at an astonishing rate. With the number of devices such as smartphones and tablets rapidly increasing, some experts are predicting that mobile shopping will overtake web sales in the near future.

A mobile-optimised site is just a version of your website aimed at device users. The difference is in the layout, navigation and the amount of information that is presented. The main advantage of m-commerce is that consumers can browse and buy whenever and wherever they want, and so you are likely to capture more sales.

The success of m-commerce has come as no surprise to some. Many big high street names, including Marks and Spencer, John Lewis and New Look, were amongst the first to invest heavily in their own mobile shopping sites and apps, and some of their sales accomplishments have been well publicised.

Customer Expectations

Expectations of m-commerce are developing as quickly as the technology. The current variety of screen sizes, resolutions and device capabilities has really put pressure on designers to produce cutting edge sites.

However, the majority of mobile shoppers are using their devices predominantly to research products, so your mobile site should focus on providing the right amount of product information, FAQs and contact details. A call now button or Live Chat facility will enable customers to get in touch instantly, which is what this technology is all about.

Some users, once they have browsed for products on a mobile site, prefer to buy online via a desktop site. You must therefore try to achieve brand cohesion between these platforms, so that customers know they are dealing with the same business. Furthermore, your existing customers will expect the same brand experience that they get from your other channels, so you'll need to work out the best way to deliver this within the constraints of mobile.

Whether your users are shopping or just gathering information, your site should have a clear search function and a menu to make it easy to navigate around your site. Above all, it's essential to make reassurances about your payment security and the protection of personal details, if you want to capture sales from the users who are comfortable buying via smartphones or tablets.

Costs

Many of the costs associated with e-commerce (discussed in chapter 3.2), such as payment acceptance, advertising, and postage and packaging, are the same for m-commerce.

Dedicated or Responsive?

There are two options available if you wish to offer m-commerce to customers. The first is a mobile dedicated site, which uses device detection to send visitors to a separate mobile site. This tends to be cheaper than the second option, which is to have a responsive site that changes to display optimally across all the viewport sizes, no matter what device (smartphone, tablet or desktop) is being used.

If you already have an ecommerce site it may be difficult to justify the expense of a responsive redesign, although many ecommerce platforms now offer a responsive site or a dedicated mobile site as part of their plans. Having a mobile site that is integrated with your existing ecommerce site means you won't have to spend time managing and updating two back offices. If, on the other hand, you are in the process of starting up, then you are in the ideal position of being able to design a mobile site at the same time as your website. When all possibilities are open to you, you can choose the most cost effective without constraint.

Design

Launching a truly unique mobile site, which has all the features you want, will probably require the services of a designer. Generally, it costs less to get an m-commerce site created than it does an e-commerce website.

It is possible to launch a mobile site without having to do any design work or coding yourself, by signing up to a provider such as MyMcart. These providers charge a monthly or annual fee, so you might want to test the water with a more basic, non-commerce mobile site first.

Whichever solution you choose, your mobile site must have simple navigation and be viewable on all of the main mobile operating systems, such as Apple iOS (for iPhones and iPads), Windows Phone, Blackberry, and Android.

Because mobile site design is still very much in its infancy and technological capabilities are constantly improving, it is likely that you'll have to update your m-commerce site in the near future.

Competition

A large number of independent jewellery and accessory retailers are yet to take advantage of the growing number of hand-held devices. A mobile-optimised site would therefore give your business an edge over any competitors that are behind the times. However, your m-site or app must be visually appealing and functional if you want to compete with the big players, who have familiar brand names and the budgets to keep up with the advances in the technology.

Some experts have forecast pure, mobile-only businesses starting up in the future. While this is unlikely, you could suddenly find yourself competing with some new names in the jewellery and accessories market.

Profitability

Whilst user confidence is growing, current sales via mobile-optimised sites are still relatively low compared to ecommerce. If you are looking for an immediate sales boost, then launching a mobile commerce site is probably not the answer, as there is a long way to go before consumers completely embrace mobile shopping. Until that happens, a mobile site will provide kudos, convenience for tech-savvy customers, and an edge over the competition. You may find you have greater success with m-commerce if your customer base is young, as this group tends to be more accustomed to using new technology.

The set-up costs for a mobile site are less than for those of a traditional e-commerce site, but you'll still need to invest in a conventional website, as customers will be more comfortable buying from your mobile store if they see that you have a 'proper' site and have bought from you before.

Even if a customer doesn't place an order using a device, your m-site can still play at part in the buying process, so its contribution to your marketing effort and overall profit shouldn't be underestimated.

In the long-term, investing in a mobile site now will pay dividends for your business in the future, as you will be able to establish a wider customer base.

Sales Channels: e-Marketplaces

E-marketplaces can be a profitable stand-alone sales channel for the jewellery and accessories retailer. They can also be a good launch pad for the fledgling business, a quick and easy way to get rid of old stock for the existing business, and a great way to test products on a small scale before launching a full-blown jewellery boutique or website.

For many customers, an e-marketplace is often the first place they visit whenever they need to buy something. Customers use them to compare products, prices and features, and very often end up completing a purchase without searching elsewhere.

The most popular e-marketplace is the online auction site eBay, but there are other outlets such as Amazon, Ebid, Etsy (for handmade items), notonthehighstreet.com (for largely British made items from small businesses) and even Facebook, which are equally suited to selling jewellery pieces and accessories.

Customer Expectations

People who shop on websites such as eBay and Amazon like to find exactly what they want, quickly and easily. You must ensure that your listings are complete, with full product details and description tags, so that people can find your items with ease when they narrow their search. Customers value convenience, so offering a fast delivery service, as well as logical navigation round your shop will aid your success.

Customers like to verify a seller's performance before they make a purchase, by checking their feedback ratings. To encourage positive feedback, and therefore future sales, you'll need to provide excellent customer service, accurate product descriptions, and be able to deliver on time. Customers are reassured when they see clear information about a seller's business, so be sure to provide your contact details and perhaps even a short description of what you do. Fair, customer-orientated policies give people further confidence.

Finally, customers who shop on auction sites like to believe that they are getting a bargain, so try to mention the RRP or original price of your product in the description, and state how much money they will save by buying from you.

Costs

Registration

The set up costs of this sales channel are generally minimal as it is free to register for most auction sites. If you subscribe to upgrades such as a shop, featured listings, or statistical reports, these will increase your outgoings each month, but are worth considering if you think they will help you sell more or increase buyer confidence.

Listing Templates

You may wish to use a template for your listings in order to stand out from the competition, and present your product information in a more appealing way. Auction site eBay, (which appears to be moving away from templates in an attempt to create cleaner pages,) charge a little extra for using their listing templates, but you can buy an off-the-shelf template or get one built for you. There are free templates available too, although you may have to change the HTML code if you want the template to match your own branding. These free templates sometimes contain adverts, but you may be able to remove them by tweaking the code.

Some experts have suggested that using a template may prevent customers from finding the listing, because a marketplace's search engine function can't infiltrate the HTML code (at least this seems to be the case with eBay's Cassini engine). What is more, many templates don't look great on mobile devices. You can find out what will work best for your business with an A/B test, where you list two versions of the same listing (one plain, one with a template) and see which gets the highest bids or number of sales.

Photographic Equipment

They say that a picture tells a thousand words, and in categories that have hundreds or even thousands of listings (and there aren't many jewellery and accessory product categories that don't), it is vital that your product images are of the highest quality. This means large, bright images that show the product accurately and truthfully. To achieve this, you will need a good camera; anything from eight mega pixels upwards should be good enough.

You should try to take images in natural daylight, although you may prefer to invest in a light tent, which is a relatively cheap piece of equipment that will eliminate shadows and provide a standard background for your images.

Photo Editing

Even with a good camera and the right lighting conditions, the images you take may still require improvement. Although you should never over-edit an image, a photo-editing program such as Photoshop will allow you to crop, brighten and remove imperfections, and make your images stand out from your competitors' images in the search results.

Listing Fees

Depending on which e-marketplaces you use, you may be charged for listing items or it may be free. Most sites charge a sales commission when you sell a product so you should calculate this before you set your price.

Postage and Packaging

The major cost associated with this channel is postage and packaging. Sellers can choose whether to offer 'free' P+P and incorporate it into the selling price (and thus avoid the risk of receiving negative feedback for high postage charges,) or to charge it separately. Some e-marketplaces put a cap on how much postage you can charge. You should experiment to find the best solution for your market.

Using a tracked service will protect you if a piece of mail gets lost in the system, or if you get a dishonest buyer, but this will obviously increase your costs.

Many of the large carriers offer discounts to companies that send a high volume of mail each week. Even if you don't yet qualify for a business account, it can be a goal you can work towards, as the savings can be significant.

Competition

Competition in the jewellery and accessories departments of e-marketplaces can be fierce and this can drive down prices. Sellers must gain a competitive advantage with unique products, customer-orientated policies, excellent customer service, and by building up positive feedback. Good product listing presentation, including high quality photos and well-written descriptions, can be the deciding factor when customers are determining which seller to buy from.

Possibly the biggest threat is the increasing number of manufacturers (many of them from the Far East) selling direct to consumers via e-marketplaces. It is impossible to compete on price with these outfits, but if you are able to offer customised, personalised, one-offs, or limited-addition items, you can charge a premium price and generate a profit. The quality of a product is the main concern customers have when buying from abroad. If appropriate, try to emphasise the design, origin and craftsmanship of your products, and consider offering buyers a warranty.

By being based in the UK, you can offer a much faster delivery service than foreign competitors. Although this raises prices for customers, there are plenty of people willing to pay a higher price in order to receive their items within a more reasonable time frame.

On Etsy, a lot of shop owners rely solely on the traffic that the site receives naturally. If you do this though, it is likely that customers will find you by doing a product search, where your listings will be competing with many others. However, if you can send traffic directly to your shop you can circumvent the competition, and you will be much more likely to gain customers. One way to generate direct traffic is by developing relationships with influential bloggers and reviewers by sending them samples and getting them to post a link to your e-marketplace shop.

Profitability

You can start selling on e-marketplaces for very little money upfront, but listing fees and sales commission can eat into your profit. It is, therefore, important to calculate a selling price that will deliver a profit, before you list any products.

Knowing exactly when your potential customers are browsing and ordering, and then running your listings to coincide with these peak times, can be a key factor in your success in an e-marketplace. 9pm is a popular shopping time, but of course it all depends on when *your* target market is visiting these sites. If you are selling on Etsy, try to stagger your listings, as this will increase your visibility on the site.

Although the aim of a sales channel is to make a profit, it doesn't always have to generate revenue directly. Some sellers are unable to make adequate money through online marketplaces, and instead use their auction listings merely as cheap adverts that send traffic to their online store, (where they are able to offer a larger range and their overheads are much lower.) Some businesses build large mailing lists through selling loss leaders on e-marketplaces. They then recuperate their losses by promoting other products and services to these customers. So, never underestimate the marketing value of a listing.

Sales Channels: Mail Order

The mail order catalogue in its traditional form is dying out. This is largely due to our changing social and shopping habits, and the rising costs of paper, printing and postage. Catalogues may still have a place in jewellery and accessory retailing though, albeit in a more modern form.

Some companies provide a downloadable or a flash 'click and flick' catalogue via their website, to satisfy the growing number of tablet users, and the people who prefer to print off and read a hard copy.

An in-store catalogue is a convenient way to offer a large product range without having to stock all of the items. It is an ideal solution for premises that are short on space, or when offering a complete product range poses a logistical problem (as in the case of exhibitors who can transport only a limited selection of products in their vehicles.)

Customer Expectations

Just as the delivery method for the catalogue has changed, so too have the expectations of those who buy from them. People expect more than just a list of the products that you offer. Look books, which are popular in the fashion world, advise readers what products work together and what items they need to buy to achieve a particular look. These 'catalogues' are packaged as magazines and present the products in an exciting and helpful way, which simultaneously exploits cross-selling. Whatever your approach, your catalogue should be easy to read, and have an appealing layout with clearly labelled products. You should make it as easy as possible for customers to find ordering information, by placing these details on every page.

One of the benefits of publishing a catalogue is that it provides customers with an alternative shopping experience; it enables them to view your range in the comfort of their own home or on the move via a device. If you operate other channels, customers will be expecting to see the same range of products available from those, and maybe even additional products if the range you have is limited.

Customers like to have the choice of either downloading a catalogue, viewing it online, or reading a hard copy, (although due to concerns about the environment and the increasing popularity of electronic devices, more people are opting for the electronic versions.)

Costs

Design

You can create a catalogue in-house with a software programme such as Microsoft Publisher or Serif Page Plus. The great thing about doing it yourself (apart from the zero outlay,) is that you can easily modify the 'template' document and save it as a PDF file whenever you need to publish a new edition of your catalogue.

If you want to hire a designer to create a catalogue for you, you'll need to be sure that you'll have enough readers to justify the expense.

Printing

If you want to have a printed catalogue, you will need to explore the different paper, printing and binding costs. For small quantities, it will probably be most cost effective to print them off on your office printer, but if you have a large number of catalogues with many pages, it may be better to get them professionally printed. The quality of the finished product may be the deciding factor though, as there is no point in producing a catalogue that looks inferior, as it just won't do the job of selling your products.

Distribution

The method you use to distribute your catalogue can have a significant impact on your expenditure. Emailing the catalogue to your mailing list or offering it for download via your website is free, and customers always have the option of printing it themselves if they want a hard copy. If you decide to post your catalogue, the cost can be astronomical, and that is before you've sent them to any overseas customers.

If you have an in-store catalogue that is never removed from your shop (just like in Argos stores), your costs will probably be much lower, especially if you produce the catalogue in-house on your PC. The cost of getting the pages laminated or presenting them in a display book is also minimal.

Mailing List

An established business with a large customer database will obviously have less trouble distributing an e-catalogue than a new business will. A mail-order company that is just starting out may need to buy a mailing list or wait until a sizeable customer base is built before launching a catalogue. If you can find another business that is looking to launch a catalogue aimed at the same demographics, you could explore the possibility of producing a joint publication and reaching more people.

Competition

A catalogue can be a useful tool that promotes your products outside of opening hours, away from your shop or stall. Because few jewellery and accessories retailers offer a catalogue alongside their other channels, it can help you stand out amongst the competition. Catalogues can be beneficial during working hours too. At a show or a shop you may be limited by space, but with a catalogue you can offer a much wider product range than competitors with the same or a larger floor space. However, companies planning to launch a pure mail order business could struggle to compete without a familiar and trusted brand name.

Profitability

Mail order is not one of the most popular ways of buying jewellery and accessories, but it can facilitate sales that you would otherwise miss out on because a customer either prefers to shop offline or has little time to visit your shop.

If you can find locations where there is demand but little supply, a catalogue can be extremely profitable for you. In remote areas, where there is poor internet connectivity and no stores nearby, a catalogue may be the only way customers can shop for accessories. If you find such a location, do thorough research beforehand to make sure there will be enough buyers to make it viable.

As previously mentioned, the cost of launching a mail order channel can be substantial, particularly if you choose to distribute printed catalogues. Thorough research is essential so that you can discover whether there is a high enough demand for shopping in this way, and whether you'll recoup your costs and make a profit. Creating an e-catalogue rather than hard copies can greatly reduce your costs and the risk.

By having an in-store catalogue that features a much wider range than your shop will allow, along with your less popular niche products, you'll reduce the amount of money you have tied up in stock and improve your cash flow.

It can sometimes be difficult to measure the revenue contribution of a catalogue, since customers may consult one during the buying process but then order via another medium such as by phone. One way to measure the success rate is to include a discount code with your catalogue, which often has the additional benefit of increasing sales.

Sales Channels: Direct Selling

For a long time, direct selling was the realm of Tupperware, Avon and window sales reps. Today, direct sellers showcase all manner of products, including jewellery and accessories, to people in their homes and at their workplaces.

Selling directly through home parties, a travelling shop, sample boxes, or door-to-door, can be a highly fulfilling and lucrative method of retailing your products. It can also help you establish yourself within your community, and is an excellent complement to the other sales channels. If you have produced your own range of jewellery and accessories, but are struggling to get retailers to stock them, then direct selling may be the best method of distribution.

Home Parties

The home party is an ever-growing retail channel, in which sellers demonstrate and promote products in someone's home or other location. The guests, plied with a glass of wine and in familiar company, are usually in a receptive frame of mind to buy.

To be a good home party host, you will need to be confident when talking to small groups of people and passionate about jewellery and accessories. You don't have to be a hard seller. In fact, it is a bonus if you are not because guests will warm to you better and buy more. The best home party sellers are able to gauge their audience and modify their tone and sales tactics accordingly.

Door-to-Door

Going door-to-door can be a demoralising exercise for business owners, and is seldom welcome by a home's occupiers. The method may work well for window sales reps; after all, everyone has windows, so a salesperson is bound to generate at least one lead. Not everyone will be interested in buying jewellery and accessories though, and even less will trust a seller at their door. Furthermore, the value of any sales you make are unlikely to justify the time and effort that you spend knocking on doors. If prospects can book a visit from you online or over the phone you may have greater success.

Don't rule out this method entirely though. If you target the right neighbourhood and get your timing right, (just before Christmas or mother's day for example,) door-to-door can be another string in your bow.

You don't necessarily have to stick to residential addresses. You may find that in places where there are larger numbers of people, such as at businesses and community groups, you can generate lots of sales. (Although, arranging to leave a sample box or host a party may be a more suitable approach to take with these.)

The Drop-off Sample Box

The sample box is a method of direct selling that has been used successfully by book, gift and confectionery companies for many years.

By putting a selection of jewellery in a box, and then leaving it with a company (with their agreement, of course), you can reach busy workers who struggle to find the time to shop. Your products will be a welcome distraction in an office or staff canteen, and once one staff member has placed an order, it often motivates their colleagues to so the same. After a week or so, you can return to collect your box and, hopefully, plenty of orders (especially if you have timed the delivery of the box to coincide with payday or an event such as Christmas!)

The Travelling Shop

Loading up a van with products, and regularly visiting locations such as markets or village squares, is another way you could enter direct selling. A sales van may work particularly well in remote areas, where the only other choices that customers have are to buy online, or to travel many miles to the nearest town.

The travelling shop is different from attending events (see chapter 3.7), as it involves building a customer base (by advertising and word of mouth,) rather than relying on passing trade. With a mobile shop comes flexibility and freedom; if a pitch is not profitable you can move on to somewhere else, and even visit multiple locations in the same day to maximise your income.

You usually need to obtain a street trading licence from the local council, which will stipulate the days and times you can trade at a specific location.

Customer Expectations

Some of the other sales channels lack the personal interaction that customers get via direct selling. Direct selling offers an alternative, sociable shopping experience, and in the case of home parties, entertainment as well. Generally, you'll need a lively, outgoing personality to be able to sell face-to-face, or persuade organisations to accept your sample box.

You should give customers enough time to look at the products, but not so much time that they change their minds about placing an order with you, which can be a risk if you undertake the drop-off sample box option.

Try to provide the same level of service that you do in your other sales channels (if you operate others), and aim to deliver products as soon as possible after a customer has placed an order. This will increase customer satisfaction and make people more likely to recommend you to their friends and colleagues.

Whichever direct selling method you use, customers will expect you to visit regularly throughout the year with new products. If you are a party seller, then they will also expect a different sales presentation each time, with advice on the latest styles.

Business cards and other marketing materials are essential. Customers will feel less pre-purchase anxiety if they have your full contact details, and know they can get in touch with you if there is a problem.

Costs

Advertising

For door-to-door and sample box selling, advertising probably isn't applicable, but for the party planner, some sort of publicity will be crucial. Spreading the word to generate bookings doesn't have to be a major cost if you can take advantage of social networking and other cheap advertising methods. (More on this in Chapters 7 and 8.)

You will probably need a vehicle to operate this sales channel. With some branded decals you can transform your motor into a mobile advert and create a professional image at the same time.

Travel

Travel costs can be high depending on the locations of the parties you host or the businesses and groups you visit. You'll need to inform your insurance provider if you start using your car for business purposes.

Vehicle maintenance and repairs will add to your costs too. An unsuccessful party or sample box can be costly if you have travelled a long way, which is why these costs in particular should be explored in advance.

Delivery

You need to think about how you will deliver items to the consumer if you don't have the products with you when you accept orders. Delivering orders in your own vehicle will probably be cost effective in your local area, but you might want to consider using a courier to deliver to customers further afield. Packing supplies need to be calculated if you plan to post orders to your customers.

Marketing Materials

Most of the aforementioned methods of direct selling will require marketing materials and stationery such as business cards, order forms, receipts and price lists. You might also need brochures and invitations for guests if you are running home parties.

Most customers will appreciate seeing your contact details on these materials, in case they have a problem, or they need to place an order before your next visit. Furthermore, customers may pass these details on to people that they know, so it is definitely worth investing in quality printed marketing literature.

Wastage

Inevitably, there will be some damage if you are displaying products in a sample box or allowing customers to try products on at home parties. Wastage is a legitimate cost that you need to accept before starting up a direct sales channel.

Competition

Most mid to large jewellery and accessories companies don't utilise direct selling methods enough, if at all, so there is definitely an opportunity for independents to succeed here.

At home parties, your jewellery and accessories will be the only that are available, and unless guests use their smartphones during the event to compare prices, you'll have no competition. With the sample box method you may face a little more competition, since you'll need to give the workers at least a few days to place orders, in which time they could check online stores, shops and supermarkets for cheaper alternatives.

Profitability

The start-up costs are relatively small, but direct selling can be a hit and miss enterprise. You may find that you struggle to make sales at some gatherings, but easily make a profit at others. Timing is everything. A sample box that you leave at a company may not generate any orders unless it's near payday, while selling parties at a local social group may only produce a profit once per season. To identity the most lucrative locations and times, you should do comprehensive research, and look at the sales data you have from any previous direct selling ventures. As you gain experience, you will find that you recoup your ongoing costs, such as fuel, much more easily.

The biggest advantage of direct selling is that it offers convenience. You'll be taking products straight to buyers, which is something that will be greatly appreciated by busy customers, especially near Christmas (the busiest time for jewellery and accessories retailers).

Direct selling can also be an opportunity to cross promote your other sales channels or services, such as jewellery cleaning and repairs, to further increase profit. If you are purely a direct seller, then perhaps you could join forces with a non-competing business and promote both businesses together.

A travelling shop can serve a community and bring people together. Rather than relying on passing trade, it helps if you publicise your visits beforehand so people know when and where you'll be visiting. As long as you can keep your advertising costs to a minimum you can make a very good profit this way.

Your door-to-door sales are likely to be higher if prospective customers request a visit from you, rather than if you cold-call them. Although some customers will feel obliged to buy whether you have an appointment or not, many people distrust unsolicited salespeople, so marketing it as a free personal shopping service may improve the uptake and generate revenue.

By combining door-to-door with a good quality catalogue (à la Betterware and Avon), you may find more prospects buy from you. In fact, whatever direct method(s) you choose, reassuring customers that you are a genuine and trustworthy business will be the key to your profitability.

Sales Channels: Events

S elling via events is no ordinary sales channel. It can be the sole channel for a full-time or part-time business, part of a multi-channel strategy, or as a marketing tactic to raise brand-awareness.

The term 'events' covers so many possibilities. You could exhibit at specific jewellery shows such as the Desire Jewellery Fair, or general events such as county shows, gift and craft events, flower shows, markets, local bring and buy sales, and school fetes. You can choose to exhibit locally, nationally, or even internationally.

It is the flexibility of this channel that is particularly appealing, as you get to choose exactly when, where, and how often to attend events. It is also a great way to meet the customers and do some competitor-research at the same time. Don't assume that it's easy money though; there are often long days on your feet, hours of preparation, and for some, cold nights spent sleeping in a van.

Costs

Stand Hire

Generally, the larger and more popular an event, the more expensive the square feet will be to hire. This should not deter you from selling at big events though. Quite often, the high footfall and the quality of visitor will ensure that you get a good return on your investment.

In contrast, hiring a stand at smaller 'local' events may cost very little, and some may even be free, but you need to be certain that there will be enough people through the doors willing to buy your products to make it worthwhile. Smaller events are a good way to learn the ropes, and the right ones will reap a nice financial reward for you as well.

To reduce the cost of hiring a trade stand you could consider joining forces with another business, although preferably one not retailing jewellery and accessories. Be aware though that some organisers will frown upon this practice and may try to get you and your 'business partner' to pay the full rate.

Exhibition Display & Signage

Some events, such as those that take place in church halls and schools, may provide a table gratis for you to display your wares, in which case you may only need to invest in a table covering and perhaps some professional banners with your brand printed on. Most event organisers hire out a space and nothing more, leaving you to dress up your designated exhibition area from scratch. If you have a tight budget, and are faced with trying to compete with your rivals' professionally customised displays, then you may need to rely on some creativity to help your stand to stand out.

If you can design, transport, and erect the stand at the venue yourself, this will keep your costs down. However, if at any point exhibiting at events becomes a larger and more serious venture for you, then you may need to hire an exhibition contractor or borrow a few willing friends to assist you.

Travel Costs

Whether you decide to exhibit locally, nationally, or internationally, there will be travel expenses involved. Obviously, the further away an event, the higher these costs are likely to be.

The one thing every exhibitor needs is a vehicle that is big enough to carry all of the stock needed, as well as any display equipment. Whether you have your own van, borrow or hire one, remember that any costs such as fuel, insurance, and maintenance, all need to be recuperated before you can break even.

Accommodation

If an event is being run over more than one day, or if it is too far away for you to drive back at the end of the night, then you'll need to arrange accommodation. The organiser of an event can usually provide a list of local hotels and B&B's, and some establishments may offer discounts to visitors and exhibitors. However, some exhibitors choose to spend one or two uncomfortable nights sleeping in their vehicle, rather than have yet another expense to eat into their profit. Your expensive stock may be safer with you on board but your personal safety should always come first.

Marketing Materials

Marketing materials, such as business cards and flyers, can reassure prospective customers that you are genuine and that they can get in touch with you if there is a problem. By providing your details on printed literature, you can also capture sales from customers who may need to check measurements, or research your business further before they buy.

Staff

At exhibitions, the flow of visitors can undulate. One minute there can be nobody in sight because everyone is watching a demonstration, the next minute there can be a huge crowd around you. At small events, you will probably be able to deal with the visitors single-handed without missing out on any sales. However, at larger events you may need more staff to reel in as many visitors as possible. If you have to hire extra staff for an event, you should make sure that they have prior experience of selling face-to-face, and understand the aims of being there.

Following-up Leads

You should follow up enquiries with mail-shots or phone calls, within a few days of an event. Obviously this could add to your costs if you follow-up via any method other than email, but the rewards can be great. Even by making just brief contact with prospects you will be ahead of your competitors, since some businesses never use the details they gather at events, and those that do, leave it so long that the visitors have usually forgotten all about them.

Customer Expectations

Many people visit exhibition shows looking for ideas and solutions, to be entertained, to learn something new, or to be the first to see an innovative product.

Those that attend with the principal intention of shopping are obviously easier to sell to, but you can still capture sales from those that haven't considered opening their wallets, by fulfilling or exceeding their expectations. At a gift fair for example, visitors will expect to see the sort of jewellery and accessories that they can give to their friends and family. You'll probably need gift boxes, and if you can offer a free gift-wrapping service as well you'll be adding value and exceeding customer expectations. At a craft event, visitors might expect to see handmade and locally inspired pieces, but hearing from the designer in person about how a piece was created may be the bonus that secures more sales. Adapting your product offering to suit the event and visitor expectations in this way shouldn't be too difficult, providing you have selected the right event for your business in the first place.

In addition to anticipating customer needs, preparation is key to a successful event. Prices should be clearly marked on every item to save you from having to repeatedly answer the same question: 'How much is this?' and to avoid losing customers that don't like to ask. Visitors may have questions about your products, or may seek your advice about how to accessorise a particular outfit, and will expect you and your staff to be knowledgeable.

Competition

The level of competition you encounter will depend largely on the type of events that you attend. At a jewellery-specific event, all of the other stands will be jewellery-related and therefore competition will be intense. At general events, your competitors will all be vying for visitors' attention, and although not every visitor will be a potential customer, you may be the only business selling jewellery and accessories and therefore have a much greater chance of standing out.

Exhibitors are facing rising competition from the internet, with visitors using smartphones to compare prices and work out the best deal. To prevent this, you must offer something different, more valuable, or use persuasion to get them to buy there and then.

The location of your stand within a venue is an important contributor to your competitiveness. If you have a permanent market pitch, it can be an advantage to be in a prominent position, near to the entrance perhaps, and where your regular customers know exactly where to find you. However, at an impermanent event, a visitor might spot something they like within minutes of entering an exhibition hall, but be reluctant to buy it in case they see something better at another stand. By the time they reach the exit, the prospect may have run out of money or forgotten all about the item. If you can get a stand near to one of the cash machines that are installed at most big events, you will have at least reduced one of the barriers to buying, namely a lack of available cash. It is better if you accept card payments and advertise this fact.

By signing up to an event early, you may have more choice in the location of your stand. Organisers will sometimes provide a map of the layout, which will make it easier for you to pick a good position. The location of the largest companies that will be exhibiting can be easily identified, as these usually take up the biggest stands and the islands. Should you try to avoid having a booth right next to a well-known competitor? The benefits of being positioned near a more popular stand tend to outweigh the drawback of being repeatedly overlooked by visitors making a beeline for them. At the very least, it is better than being stuck in a quiet corner of a venue where there is low footfall.

Friendly, approachable staff, that actively engage with visitors, will have significantly more success than staff that allow potential customers (including those that don't show any obvious interest) to walk past. Sometimes all it takes is a friendly 'hello' to hook a customer, and if your competitors aren't doing this then you will have a massive advantage.

Profitability

Due to the cost of exhibition displays, your start-up costs may be high. You may be able to break-even and make a good profit after one big jewellery event, but attending shows regularly may be the only way to ensure that this sales channel is worth the initial preparation and effort.

Ongoing costs such as fuel can cancel out any revenue you generate, so selecting the right events is crucial. Your primary research is an important starting point because it will identify the events that your target market are likely to visit, and how much they are likely to spend. You should then find out as much as you can about the actual events, as there are certain factors that will affect visitor numbers and sales. An entry fee, for instance, might limit visitor numbers, but it ensures that the people who visit are genuinely interested in the event and are willing to spend money. A free event may attract people who are just looking for a day out and have no intention of spending money. Other factors such as transport links, the size of the venue, and the age of the event could also be looked into.

The type of event that you stand at, whether general or accessories-specific, will affect the quality of the visitor you encounter and thus the volume of sales. Where and how the organisers are publicising the event may give you an idea of whether enough people from your target market will be attending. A final clue about an event's potential profitability may come from finding out the events that your competitors are attending, or not re-attending, as the case may be.

In the next chapter, we will discover the importance of creating a strong brand identity, and how the right branding can attract more customers.

Branding and Brands

Business experts often talk about brands and branding as if they are the same thing. While the two are related, they are actually very different.

Branding is the collection of unique visual identifiers (such as your logo and colourway) that makes your business attractive and instantly recognisable. Your brand, on the other hand, is your business's personality, and is based largely on how the public perceive your company.

A customer will always choose a business with attractive branding and a consistent brand, over a business that doesn't appear to have invested much time or thought into it. Poorly executed branding not only makes a company and its products look unappealing, it may raise questions in the customers mind about what other areas of the business may be poorly implemented.

Developing Your Branding

I f you are a start-up business, then you are in the advantageous position of being able to look at the whole picture before you go ahead and perhaps brief a graphic designer, or get ten thousand flyers printed.

Figure 4.1 How branding can be developed

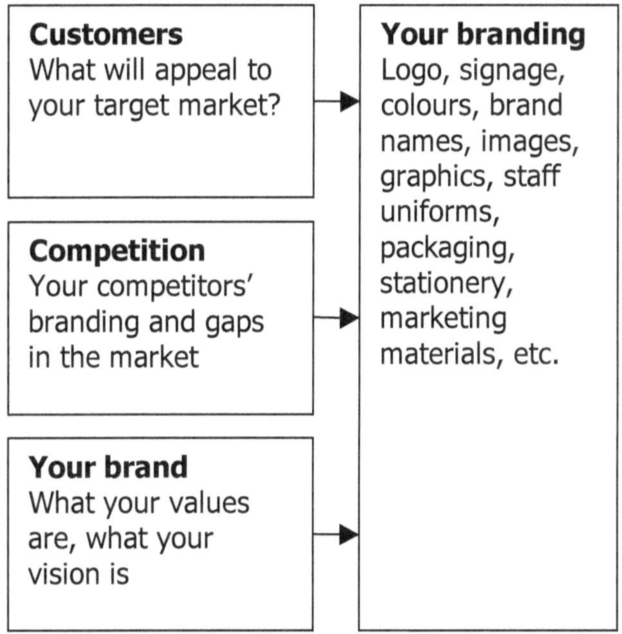

Figure 4.1 above shows that your customers, the competition and your brand, play a huge part in developing your branding. Exploring each one will help you decide how your branding should look.

Customers

When it comes to designing branding, the most important thing you need to consider is what will appeal to your customers. You may have to make a few assumptions about the designs that will resonate with them, but this should always be based on your own market research findings. Factors such as age, income, occupation, lifestyle, education, religion, and location, can have an effect on how your target market responds to your branding.

Age and Family Life Cycle

It is essential to consider the ages of your target market and their current stage in the life cycle, as it can influence the sort of branding that appeals to them. During a person's life there will be a number of events and changing circumstances, which will affect the sort of jewellery and accessories they buy. A young male, for example, may buy gifts for his girlfriend and female members of his family. As he gets older he may buy an engagement ring and then wedding rings. When he matures he'll buy anniversary gifts, and birthday gifts for his wife and children. Targeting people in any one of these stages may require a very specific style of branding.

Income

The average income of your target customers (their job title can give you a general idea) is an important consideration when planning your branding. Upmarket branding that implies that your products and prices are above a customer's budget can be off-putting, although, it can increase desirability for those products. Similarly, if your target market is earning above a certain income level, they might view a discount 'cheap n cheerful' style as a step backwards. Perhaps more important than salary, is the amount of discretionary income (or money left over after the household bills have been paid) that people have to spend on themselves. A family may have a high household income but mum could be left with little discretionary income to spend on jewellery and accessories. In contrast, a retired female could have less income, but, because the mortgage is paid and she has no dependants living at home, she may have more money to spend on herself.

Gender

The gender of your target market could affect elements of your branding. If your target market is principally one gender, then you can create highly focused branding that will appeal to them. Females generally prefer softer lines and colours, whilst males prefer more masculine styles and darker colours. If your target market is made up equally of both genders, then you may want to choose a more gender-neutral colour scheme for your branding. Of course, these are not steadfast rules, and you should be careful not to stereotype.

Geographical Location

The sales channels you operate will largely determine the geographical locations you target. Your business can be local (e.g., a stall at a local gala) or have a much broader reach (e.g., an online shop).

If your target market is 'local' i.e., they reside or work within one area, city, or county, then they may appreciate a reference to the locale in the brand name, or the inclusion of a local landmark in the logo. Being proudly local doesn't have to be restrictive if you later decide to export. Companies such as Links of London and Macintyres of Edinburgh have successfully managed to capitalise on the desirability of their location by incorporating it in their names.

However, the owners of businesses that have a wider reach, such as internet shops, will need to do their research, as some colours or symbols may be seen as unlucky or offensive in certain cultures. Furthermore, a local reference or a play on words that requires special knowledge to be understood, could confuse a customer from another country, so, unless it is world-renowned, exercise caution.

Behaviour & Lifestyle

There are many lifestyle and behavioural factors you may have to take into account when designing your branding.

If your target market regularly purchase upscale jewellery and accessories for example, then it is likely that they also spend a lot of money on other luxury items. Luxury brands typically share the same characteristic: they are aspirational, and therefore you can look to the other labels that they buy for inspiration for your own aspirational branding.

The enduring obsession people have with celebrities is another behaviour that may need to be reflected in your branding. If your customers look to famous people for style ideas, then a logo or a tag line that acknowledges this will tell customers that yours is a brand for them.

If you have a young target market for whom looking stylish is a top priority, then energetic and stylish branding is likely to appeal to them more than branding that exudes a classic, timeless air.

The emergent pre-teen market can be captured with bright, colourful and catchy branding, which not only strikes a chord with the children, but is also parent-friendly to exploit pester power.

Competition

Branding helps to create a desired perception of a business, its products and people. It can reassure customers that you have the same, or better, capabilities as your competitors and can deliver on your promises.

In your market research, you should have examined the branding that your competitors use to attract customers. The colours, logos, imagery, themes and styles used by your rivals may give you ideas for the look and feel of your own branding. However, it is more important that you find any gaps that competitors have left. Anything that helps you stand out from the rest and attract customers will ultimately increase your profit. Perhaps there is a colourway that is currently not in use, or perhaps your competitors all share a similar theme, and therefore, there is an opportunity for something very different. In saturated markets, it may be quite difficult to find a gap. However, there could still be an opportunity to differentiate your business by taking a concept that is already in use and executing it in a better way. Maybe one of your rivals has a 'Hollywood Glamour' theme, but they have not been consistent with it. Maybe another competitor sells artisan jewellery, but it's hard to tell because their branding gives no indication of it.

Your competitors' weaknesses are an opportunity to distinguish your business by building a stronger identity through your branding. Be aware though that some gaps in the market may have been left for a reason; they simply don't work.

Your Brand

Although your logo, colour scheme, and tagline can give potential customers an idea of what to expect from your business, your brand is so much more than graphic design. After all, a logo is just a symbol, a colour scheme is a few colours put together, and a tagline is some memorable words that sum up what you do.

According to the Design Council, a brand is a set of associations that people make with a company, product, service, or individual. It is all the thoughts, ideas, feelings, and opinions that people have about you, which may be based on their previous experiences of doing business with you, the impression they get from your branding, or what their friends have told them. To be concise, it is your business's personality.

Your past and existing customers will have formed their opinions about your business based on key aspects such as your customer service, product knowledge, quality, convenience, ease of ordering, delivery, interior of shop, and ease of use of your website.

Prospective customers that have no previous experience of doing business with you, will base their decision on whether to buy your accessories purely on external information, such as word of mouth recommendations and customer review sites, as well as the first impression they get from your branding.

As we will discover in Chapter 7, by delivering excellence in the areas that are important to your customers, you can create a positive association with your brand. You'll then be positively influencing what your customers tell their friends and family, and the world on customer review sites.

Defining Your Brand

To define your brand:

1. List the characteristics of your products and services. (E.g., glamorous, stylish, innovative, pretty, value, fun, and unique.)

2. List the aims and values of your business. (E.g., to bring affordable, allergy-free jewellery and fashion accessories to the UK, to promote young designers in your local area.)

3. Define your target market. (E.g., age, lifestyle, jobs, income, and favourite style.)

4. What is your specialist area? (E.g., a particular style, age group, or material.)

5. How do you want people to perceive your business? (E.g., as a business that values its customers, is ethical, is energetic and different.)

Once you have your brand concept on paper, you should refer to it every time you are engaging in business communications such as:

- Creating business cards and flyers
- Designing the look and layout of your premises
- Writing content for your website or blog
- Designing signage
- Updating your Facebook page or Twitter account
- Answering the phone
- Talking to your staff
- Sending emails to your customers

- Writing advertising content
- Networking and engaging with the public

Ask yourself if your brand were a person how would it approach the various tasks of your business? How would it address its customers (formally or informally)? What language and tone would it use (energetic, fun, humorous, or professional)? Staying focused on who you are, and what your business stands for, will help you to achieve a strong and consistent brand throughout your company.

External Brand Perceptions

While you can influence the perception of your brand by striving for excellence in the areas that your customers value, such as quality and service, there are always going to be some things that are out of your control. For instance, a story could appear in a national newspaper about a jewellery retailer using an unethical foreign supplier that has been environmentally irresponsible. While the story might not mention your business, it might get the general public questioning whether it is right to buy cheap jewellery and accessories, and this may have a negative, albeit indirect, impact on your brand. Similarly, one company's product recall could have an effect on every other business within the industry. If a range of children's purses were recalled due to their toxicity, this may cause your customers to avoid buying all children's purses, even if you stock a different brand.

Thankfully, the effects of bad press are usually only temporary, and the chances of a full recovery are vastly improved if you have already established a strong, positive association with your brand. However, a consistent run of poor reviews and complaints can cause irreparable damage. This is one of the reasons some companies spend thousands on re-branding; it wipes the slate clean enabling them to move forward and rebuild a new, more positive image. The majority of small to medium businesses however, don't have thousands of pounds to spare if something goes wrong, so managing and maintaining your brand image will help you avoid costly re-branding exercises.

Branding

Branding is all the visual elements that make your business unique, and includes your logo, business and brand names, theme and style, signage, staff uniforms, packaging, stationery, marketing materials, and associated images and graphics. It is a visual representation of your brand. If it is implemented well, your branding will give prospective customers a clear and immediate message about who you are, what you do, and what they can expect from you in terms of quality and service. It can also provide you with a competitive advantage, as it communicates what is different about your business, and its products and services.

Branding helps to:

- Attract your target market
- Make your business look credible
- Appeal to your customers on an emotional level
- Represent your business's personality
- Increase desirability for products and services
- Motivate customers to buy
- Make a business stand out from the competition
- Make your business instantly recognisable

For new businesses that are yet to build a customer base, branding is of vital importance because prospective customers will have nothing else to go on apart from their first impressions.

Choosing a Name

Your business name is possibly the most essential aspect of any branding. If you already have a business, but think that your company name won't translate well to retail, then you may want to consider choosing a different brand name just for your jewellery and accessories range.

Some of the best business and brand names are descriptive, and may, for example, include the phrases 'jewellery boutique' or 'fashion accessories'. While abstract and made-up names can work too, it does make it harder to convey to people exactly what you do. Having an explanatory name is a bonus on the internet too, because web addresses with good descriptive keywords may rank higher on some search engines.

Don't limit yourself by being over-descriptive though. You may initially plan to supply only fashion jewellery and give yourself the name 'Bling Fashion Jewellery', but this may make it difficult for you to diversify into other areas such as fine jewellery, or handbags and fashion accessories in the future.

As previously mentioned, you can take inspiration from local landmarks or culture if you think it will appeal to your target market. While some locations are highly desirable, take care not to exclude potential customers from outside your territory.

The main challenge you will have is finding a name that is not already in use. Try searching the WHOIS directory to see if anyone has registered the domain name, and check all the major social networking sites too. Even if you don't plan to use such sites, if someone else is using your name it may cause confusion amongst customers (search 'John Lewis Twitter Man' for an example of mistaken identity.) You should also check if a name has been trademarked at ipo.gov.uk.

Once you have shortlisted a few names that are available, consider how each would look in a logo or shop sign. Is it easy to spell and pronounce? Does it give the right impression? Could it be confused with an existing company? As with most aspects of your business, you should ask the opinions of those that matter: your customers and staff.

Graphic Design

A major element of branding is graphic design. While you could commission an expensive design company, there are many freelance graphic designers available for hire on marketplaces such as Fiverr.com and Upwork.com. The best person for the job won't just be talented at graphic design, but they will have an ability to encapsulate your business and its values visually. If you have an eye for design and can use software such as Photoshop, then you could make considerable savings by doing it yourself, in-house. Be honest about your capability as a graphic designer though, because your branding needs to look professional and be as good as your competitors'.

Whether you design your own branding or hire someone to do it, you should start with a brief that outlines what your vision for your brand is, who your customers are, and what image you want the branding to communicate to the public.

Developing your ideas into workable designs, which are part of a cohesive branding proposition, takes time. Once you have come up with a few possible designs, it is a good idea to seek the opinion of your research sample again, to find out which designs they like and what impression each gives about your business. It may take a few trips back and forth between your sample and the drawing board before you get it right, but it will be worth the effort.

Branding Evolution

In time, established businesses sometimes find that their branding is no longer unique. This could be because competitors that have since entered the market have *gained inspiration* from some part of their identity. Other businesses may feel that their branding has become tired and outdated because trends have changed. If this happens to you, there is no reason why you can't make subtle updates to your existing branding. After all, some of the most iconic logos have gone through several evolutions over time, and some have ended up looking very different from their original insignia. A branding update can give a boost to customers, staff and owners.

In some circumstances, a total rebrand, (which includes a change in attitude and values,) may be necessary. You may need to start anew if you have experienced irreversible negative publicity, expanded your product offering, or diversified into new markets.

No one can deny that such a major decision should always be fully researched, not least because it can take a lot of hard work to gain customer acceptance of change. Despite this, there have been a number of cases in which some well-known companies have given their brand an expensive makeover, only to be forced to backtrack following protests from loyal fans. While these companies probably did do some research, they failed to realise just how much those particular customers loved the brand. If a business has fans of any kind then they are obviously doing something right. To avoid making this mistake yourself, you should consult a sizeable research sample before implementing any major changes. Above all, you must remember that your customers' perceptions and needs are more important than keeping up with competitor rebrands, or your own whims.

In the next chapter, we will look at the various jewellery and accessory products available, the best places to find reliable suppliers, and how to reduce the risks when importing.

5

Sourcing Products and Suppliers

Sourcing quality products from trustworthy suppliers can be an arduous task that requires much research.

When sourcing, it is important to keep in mind your overall aim; that you are looking for products that your customers want to buy, which you can sell at a profit.

Having a clear idea of the products that you need to stock, will make searching for suppliers much easier. You can narrow down your search by supplier type (e.g., manufacturer or wholesaler,) and location (e.g., the UK or overseas,) to get enhanced results and improve your chances of finding exactly what you need.

Sourcing from overseas has many benefits, but you'll need to be aware of the different payment methods and the documentation required to ensure that the process of importing runs smoothly.

Once you have a list of potential suppliers that can provide the right products, you then need to decide with which ones you want to do business. While there are great trade suppliers out there, there are also some unreliable, unscrupulous outfits that need to be avoided. Thankfully, the internet makes the task of researching and vetting suppliers fairly easy and reliable.

Products

B efore you start searching for suppliers, you need to decide what products you want to stock (Figure 5.1.) Your market research findings will tell you which markets you need to focus on, and which categories or types of products to stock. Good research will also identify the product requirements and preferences that customers have, (such as styles, colours, sizes, characteristics, and uses). This information can be used to narrow down your initial supplier search and ensure that the products you eventually stock will meet customer needs.

Searching for suppliers of 'women's handbags', for example, will yield far too many results, but if you know that your target market are city professionals, then you can assume that they will need a smart handbag for work, perhaps with compartments for their smartphone and notebook. Searching using such specifics will enable you to find a supplier more quickly.

Suppliers

Types of Suppliers

The types of supplier you choose can have an effect on minimum order quantities, lead times, margins and many other factors.

Manufacturers

Buying directly from the manufacturer is a future aim for many businesses, as unit costs are much lower when buying in bulk and you can cut out the middleman.

Manufacturers tend to impose high minimum order quantities (MOQs), either as a monetary value, or as a minimum number of pieces. As a result, purchasing from a manufacturer usually requires you to have sizeable storage space, as well as the channels in place to turn over high volumes quickly. If a large amount of money is tied up in stock for too long then you could encounter cash flow problems.

If you have designs for your own jewellery and accessories, and you plan to get them mass-produced, then it is manufacturers that you need to approach.

Wholesalers

Wholesalers buy in bulk, usually from several different manufacturers. They then break up the bulk, add their mark-up, and sell on to retailers in much smaller quantities.

If you choose to buy your stock from wholesalers, you will probably be subject to minimum order quantities, (especially if it's your first order with a company,) although, these requirements are likely to be considerably less than those imposed by manufacturers.

Drop shippers

Drop shipping is an option that allows businesses to sell without ever stocking a single product. You promote the drop-shipper's products on your website or in a catalogue, and when your customer places an order, you then order the products from the drop-shipper. Your supplier will pack and dispatch the items directly to your customer or to you (for your customer to collect in-store). Your profit is the difference between your selling price and the price you pay the drop-shipper, which typically is around 30% of the RRP.

The advantages of this are clear; you have no money tied up in stock, and you can offer a complete range of jewellery and accessories without having to find secure storage for hundreds or even thousands of products. This leaves you to focus on the all-important sales and marketing.

Figure 5.1 Product Requirements Table

Product Types	Materials	Requirements
Earrings Necklaces Pendants Rings Bracelets Charms Anklets Toe Rings Belly Chains Body Jewellery Watches Pins & Brooches Handbags Purses and wallets Scarves Belts Frames & Sunglasses Phone and bag charms Keyrings Hair accessories Hats & fascinators Tiaras Bandanas & buffs Gloves Legwear (tights, stockings, socks) Jewellery boxes, pouches & display stands	Precious metals (e.g., gold, titanium, silver, white gold, palladium, platinum, rhodium) Plated (e.g., silver, gold, rhodium) Precious gemstones (e.g., diamond, ruby, emerald, sapphire) Semi precious stones (e.g., amber, amethyst, opal, quartz, turquoise, jade, garnet) Man-made simulated and synthetic gems (e.g., rhinestone, cubic zirconia, lead crystal) Other materials (e.g., pearl, plastic, stainless steel, glass, wood, enamel, shell, polymer clay, leather, wool, cotton, nylon)	What styles, characteristics, colours, patterns and sizes are needed? Does the product need to be British-made, handmade, Fair Trade, customisable or personalised? What are the current and future fashion trends for this type of product? What level of quality and durability does your target market require? Does the product need to meet any quality standards such as ISO, be nickel-free, or hallmarked? What government and EC regulations does it need to meet? E.g., be lead free) What techniques and finishes are needed? (E.g., high polish, matte, satin, hammered, brushed, hand stitched, claw setting)

Independent Craftspeople and Designers

Since the 2008 credit crunch, there has been a surge in the number of people making their own jewellery and accessories. For many, it is a hobby or a way to save money. For others it is also a great way to make money. At the other end of the scale there are the designers and design graduates offering high-end, unique pieces.

Even if you are not creative yourself, you shouldn't overlook independent craftspeople as possible suppliers. The volumes that they are able to produce are obviously smaller than those of the manufacturers, and the production times can be much longer. Generally, buying from an independent craftsperson is a more expensive option than buying from other suppliers, mainly due to the time and love that goes into each creation. However, the products that are produced can be highly distinctive, customised, ethical, or 'local', and for this many customers are willing to pay a premium.

Location of Suppliers

The location of your suppliers can affect delivery times, product quality, communication, conditions, and costs.

UK

The manufacturing industry has diminished in the UK, so the majority of suppliers you'll find here will be wholesalers and independent craftspeople.

There are many advantages to buying from the UK rather than abroad, including faster lead times, more straightforward communication, and cheaper delivery. However, this means that you are more likely to find yourself selling exactly the same jewellery and accessories as your rivals. If a supplier is easy to find, other people can find them too.

Overseas

Sourcing overseas opens up your choices so you can benefit from expertise, craftsmanship and technology that may not be available domestically. India, Italy, the Far East, and USA, are just some of the countries you could look to for suppliers of accessories. Some countries are better at producing certain products than others, so do your research.

Using suppliers abroad may significantly reduce unit prices, but import duty, VAT and shipping costs can sometimes cancel out any savings you make.

The language barrier can be an issue too, but foreign suppliers that are serious about exporting will have a sales rep that speaks good English.

Import Basics

The one thing that puts many people off from importing, especially from outside the EU, is the thought of all the extra paperwork they'll have to do. However, it is rarely as tedious and as difficult as people imagine. In fact, your supplier (the exporter) will have to do most of the work.

When importing by sea, you'll receive a notice of arrival. If the size of your goods is Less than a Container Load (LCL) then your cargo will arrive in a groupage container, be taken to a bonded warehouse, and given a unique consignment number (UCN).

The consignment will not be released until the goods have cleared customs, and for this to happen, you will need to provide the shipping company with the Commercial Invoice, Packing List, and Bill of Lading, (which should all be provided by your supplier.)

You will also need to provide your VAT number. If you are not VAT registered, then you will need to obtain an EORI number (Economic Operator Registration and Identification) from Revenue and Customs.

Finally, you'll need to provide the ten-digit Commodity Code for your products, which you can find out at Gov.uk. The code dictates the amount of duty and VAT to be applied, so it's always wise to check this before you place an order. You should have enough funds available when the goods arrive to avoid having to pay any costly storage charges.

Figure 5.2 The Pros and Cons of Supplier Location

	PROS	**CONS**
UK	Get stock quickly Cheaper delivery costs Payment by card, Bacs, or cheque is straightforward Easy to communicate with Easy to visit Easy to contact if there is a problem Covered by UK law Low minimum order as most UK suppliers are wholesalers	Unit prices are likely to be high UK suppliers can easily supply your rivals, which could drive down prices
EUROPE	Wider choice of products and suppliers You can sell products that are different to those of your rivals Fairly easy to visit. Prices may be lower than the UK. No import duty to pay within EU Trade Zone	The language barrier Currency exchange rates can affect prices Quality standards and working conditions are not always the same as the UK Delivery times are longer Import duty and extra paperwork (for countries not in the EU)
GLOBAL	Widest choice of products and suppliers Generally cheaper prices You can get your own designs manufactured more cheaply	The language barrier Currency exchange rates can affect prices Delivery times are longest Working conditions and quality standards abroad are not the same as in the UK Import duty and extra paperwork

If you purchased the goods from your supplier "Ex Works," then you are responsible for all delivery charges from their factory to yours.

Once you have paid the import duty and other charges to the shipping company, and the goods have been cleared by customs, your consignment will be delivered to you.

In contrast, when you import by air, the carrier will usually pay the import duty and VAT on your behalf to avoid a delay at customs. You will then either have to pay these charges before the goods are delivered, or you will be invoiced within thirty days of delivery. You'll need a statement of valuation if you are importing goods that are worth more than £6500.

Importing can be straightforward, provided your supplier has presented all the necessary documentation including a Commercial Invoice stating the number of units and their value.

Payment Methods

Paying for a foreign order can be a little more complex than if you were buying from the UK. While some foreign suppliers may accept card payments, Western Union, and even PayPal, bank transfers are the most common method. SWIFT, the bank transfer system, is used to send foreign currency transfers outside the UK. You can do this through your bank, (some will let you do it online) for a fee.

Payment Terms

There are some different terms that you may come across when paying for your imports:

Letter of credit – is a form of guarantee with your bank instructing them to pay for the goods only when the supplier has produced the export documents. There is a fee for this, but it does offer protection against suppliers who do not deliver the goods.

Advance payment – is the most common payment term when importing goods, and requires you (the importer) to pay for the goods in full before the supplier ships them. This obviously carries a lot of risk for the buyer and none for the seller.

Open account trading – is basically a credit account whereby the supplier sends out the goods and the buyer pays within the agreed timeframe. Whilst this carries no risk to the buyer, it is risky for the supplier and hence is not a commonly used payment term. Open account is usually used when a large and reliable buyer needs a regular supply of stock.

Beginning Your Search

A good starting point when searching for suppliers is the internet. A basic search might produce a substantial number of results, so be specific about what you are looking for, such as, 'cubic zirconia necklaces wholesaler UK', or 'retro handbags bulk supplier', or 'nickel free charm bracelet manufacturer China.' If 'jewellery' is part of your search term, try searching using the US spelling 'jewelry', and 'ladies' as well as 'women's' as you might come across suppliers that your competitors haven't found.

Where to search for suppliers:
- Search engine results (e.g., Google)
- B2B Directories and Marketplaces (e.g., Alibaba, The Wholesaler, AliExpress, Global Sources, Busy Trade, Small Volume)
- Trade magazines and newspapers (e.g., Jewellery Focus)
- Jewellery and Accessories Trade shows (e.g. The Jewellery Show London in the UK, Bijoux in Italy, and Accessorie Circuit in the USA)
- Cash and carries (e.g., Amber Jewellery)
- Secret shopping (by visiting jewellery boutiques and making a note of the distributors' addresses on the swing tags of products.)
- Online Communities (such as business forums and LinkedIn)

- E-marketplaces (by searching for job lots from wholesalers and liquidations. In addition, some manufacturers selling on auction sites may be willing to sell in bulk if you ask.)
- Sourcing or buying agents
- Networking events can uncover suppliers that your rivals may not be aware of, including local craftspeople

Approaching Suppliers

Your first contact with a potential supplier should be to determine if they have a minimum order and the prices of their products. You should be brief and avoid negotiation until you have built up a rapport with a few emails, meetings, or phone calls.

Negotiation

It never hurts to ask a supplier if they can offer you a better price, or to suggest that one of their rivals has offered you a lower price, but that you are keen to do business with them instead. Telling a supplier that you plan to place larger orders with them in the future can also encourage a reduced price or more favourable terms, especially if it is your first order.

Shortlisting

While cost and quality are very important factors when sourcing products, there are other aspects such as reliability, ethics and packaging to consider, which can help you narrow down the possibilities.

Capability and stability - Suppliers that have been operating for years will have learned from their early mistakes and become more efficient and competent. A financially stable company is more likely to make good on their promises. Above all, a supplier needs to have the skills and experience to produce pieces to the quality and specifications you require.

How do they deal with defects? – At some point, you are bound to encounter a defective product. Will your supplier accept returns long after the initial sale? Or will you be happy to accept a small percentage of wastage caused by imperfections or faults.

Ethics and the environment – customers are becoming increasingly concerned about their carbon footprint. In an ideal world we would all source suppliers as locally as possible and reduce our customer's unease, although due to the UK's current manufacturing capabilities this may be an unrealistic aim.

Some customers like to be reassured that the products they buy have come from an ethical source where staff are treated fairly. Workers in countries such as India do not always benefit from the same employment standards as their UK counterparts. If you have an ethical target market then it is highly recommended that you visit the factories in person to see the working conditions, rather than rely on assurances given by the company.

Don't put all your eggs in one basket – You should be seeking more than one supplier. If you rely on just one, and they unexpectedly close down, it could spell disaster for your business.

Your brand or theirs? – Selling jewellery and accessories that belong to an established brand means that you can benefit from its reputation and marketing. However, if you would rather put effort into building your own brand, then you have two options. You could choose a supplier that offers a white label service and have your logo imprinted on accessories. There is often a high minimum order imposed, making this option unviable for many small independents. Alternatively, you could source unbranded products from suppliers, and either pass them off as your own or add your own branded packaging, swing tags and labels. Of course, the ultimate option would be to design your own unique range of branded products. If this is what you want to do, then you should ensure that suppliers have the right expertise to handle the job.

Exclusivity – Having exclusive rights to sell a brand in your town, county, or country, is a coup for any business. A supplier may demand regular orders, or that you meet certain criteria, before you can achieve this prestigious status.

Competition – You'll need to find out how many of your competitors are selling the supplier's products. Furthermore, a wholesaler selling direct to the public could pose a problem especially if they start lowering their retail prices.

Support – Do the suppliers offer point of sale materials, display units, and product information cards? Have they got a website or contact number for consumers, and will your details be added to their stockist list? Some suppliers will deal with your customers directly, offering them after-sales advice, and even a repair service.

Discounts – Even if you are unable to negotiate lower prices from a supplier, you may still be able to take advantage of any discount and loyalty schemes they offer. If you make frequent orders or spend large amounts, the savings you can benefit from in the long term can be better than a price reduction on your first order.

Terms – The suppliers' terms of sale, including lead times, prices, minimum order quantity, and late delivery clause, should be compared to find the fairest suppliers.

Shortlisting Potential Suppliers

Before you go ahead and part with any cash, you should thoroughly research any prospective suppliers. Obviously, the bigger the purchase you are planning to make, the more time you should spend checking them out.

Internet search – View their website or marketing literature to see what information you can glean. Check if they have genuine business premises rather than a mail-forwarding address. Read their company documents, which you can download from Companies House for a nominal fee.

Also, try Googling their company name, product, or brand along with 'complaints,' 'avoid,' 'reviews,' or 'problems', to see if anyone has had issues with them in the past.

Visit them – Visit their premises, their stand at trade shows, or telephone them to speak to the main sales rep.

Ask for samples – If you are unable to visit, then ask for samples. You may have to pay for these, although some suppliers will refund the cost of purchased samples when you place a full order.

Ask your target market – Some of your customers or potential customers may have already encountered the products you are interested in stocking, so find out what they think about the brand in your primary and secondary research, or ask questions on social networking sites.

Ask for references – Ask suppliers for a list of the people they supply, or look at their stockist's page and contact some of the businesses listed. You can also use business forums to ask if anyone has ever used a particular supplier, but be aware that by doing so you may be alerting rivals to a new supplier.

Consider supplier status and ratings – Some supplier directories and marketplaces such as Alibaba have their own vetting system, involving factory inspection and account auditing. However, a good rating doesn't mean you should automatically trust them. Consider their rating along with all their other virtues.

Read the news – Search trade magazines and business news for any evidence of financial problems within the company, such as redundancies. In contrast, recruitment adverts are a positive sign of the growth of a company.

Sourcing Agents

If you do not have the time to visit and research suppliers, but want to rely on more than just some samples sent in the post before placing an order, then hiring a buying agent might be the answer. Sourcing or buying agents will visit potential suppliers to source products, collect samples and negotiate prices on your behalf, as per your brief. Their hourly rates are often quite reasonable because on buying trips they are usually sourcing for several clients at the same time.

In the next chapter, we shall discover the pricing strategies and tactics you can use to gain a competitive advantage, and how to price your products to maximise your profit.

⑥

The Art and Science of Pricing

According to Prof Charles Toftoy, pricing is "part art and part science," and is arguably one of the hardest, yet most important tasks of any business.

Pricing can affect the way your brand and products are perceived, your sales volume, and ultimately your ability to survive. If you pitch your prices too high, no one will buy, and customers might think you are greedy. If you pitch your prices too low, you could be inundated with orders that leave you struggling to cope with demand and bring in very little profit, while your customers may wonder whether the quality is any good.

There are a number of tactics and strategies that you can use when pricing. Although the vast majority of business owners don't usually consult a textbook when determining prices for their products, this is only possible because they have an understanding of the key pricing principles and know their target market.

One 'scientific' method that can be of help is the calculation of a price *range*, rather than a single price, for each product. This approach can help you decide sale prices and discounts, as well as give you the flexibility to re-adjust the price to maximise your profit.

The Science of Pricing

B efore pricing any products, business owners need to put aside the misconception that price is the only tool that can be used to compete. Yes, it is a factor that can influence a customer's buying decision, but some independents become fixated on competing on price, particularly when they find themselves operating in the shadow of a big player, or when trying to gain market share amongst the countless online companies. They believe that customers are constantly seeking out the lowest prices, when in truth most are simply seeking *value* for money.

Benefits and Features

Although you wouldn't want to price yourself out of the market by over-charging, it is important that your price reflects the benefits, features and uniqueness of your products, such as their:

- Quality of workmanship
- Quality of materials
- On-trend style
- Multi-features
- Uniqueness of design
- Handmade, customised, or personalised features
- Origins (e.g. British-made, ethically made)
- Vintage
- Exclusive brand name
- Calibre of designer

A price that does not reflect this *extra* may be dismissed by the consumer as being too good to be true and it could have a detrimental impact on the overall perception of your brand.

Adding Value

You should take into account the ways in which you add value that have nothing to do with the product itself, such as:

- Your packaging and presentation (e.g., a gift wrapping service, gift boxes)
- Service (e.g., fast and efficient customer service, knowledgeable staff, a warm welcome, bilingual customer support)
- A convenient location and an inviting shop interior
- Guarantees (e.g., free returns, extended exchange periods)
- Delivery (e.g., express home delivery, click and collect, a gift sending service)
- Stocking a large or specialist range
- Credit terms

These factors may be hard to define in monetary terms, but they still have a value to the customer all the same.

Pricing Strategies

There are a number of pricing strategies that you could use, depending on your unique circumstances and what you aim to achieve with your jewellery and accessories business.

Prestige Pricing for Unique Businesses and Products

You can charge a higher price for products that are unique or exclusive, or if your location can justify inflated prices. For example, if you stock handmade bridal jewellery, you are the sole company licensed to sell a range of innovative briefcases, or yours is the only shop in an area that sells a sought-after brand, then you can charge a premium for your products.

Penetration Pricing for New Businesses and Products

Penetrative pricing is often used by start-ups to help establish themselves in the market. Products are initially priced low, but once a business has gained market share the price is increased. Consider this strategy carefully before you implement it because you can lose a significant number of your customer base when you hike up your prices. Furthermore, raising prices during economically challenging times is nearly always detrimental.

Economy Pricing for 'Pile Them High' Businesses

Economy pricing is a strategy that many supermarkets and multi-chain stores follow. The low selling price reflects a product's low-cost mass manufacturing, and their tiny profit margins are viable only because they sell in such high volumes. Emulating such a pricing structure rarely works for smaller companies, and it is certainly not advisable to use an economy pricing strategy simply to compete with the big players.

Price Skimming for Niche Businesses

If you have a niche market, you can charge a higher price for your jewellery and accessories. The advantage obtained from a successful niche is rarely sustainable though. It usually doesn't take long for competitors to notice that you're making lots of money, and to then start offering their own alternatives at cheaper prices. When this happens, you'll probably have to lower your price, but you should hopefully have a new niche product ready to launch and thus, your profit won't have to take a hit.

Pricing Tactics

Pricing tactics are textbook tools that you can use to achieve your overall pricing strategy. Below are four of the most common.

Optional Extras Pricing

Businesses can try to increase their customer's basket value with 'price bundling' or optional extras pricing. If a customer buys a pair of earrings for example, a bundle could include the matching necklace and bracelet at a cheaper price than if they were buying the three items separately.

Decoy Pricing

A close relative of price bundling is the decoy effect or asymmetric dominance. By offering an 'inferior' product you can increase customer preference for a 'superior' product. When presented with a set of buying options, customers tend to compare the value of items against each other rather than take into account more rational factors, such as whether a price is competitive and fair, and whether they really need additional items. Take a look at this example:

Set of options A:

Earrings £20

Necklace and earrings £35

Set of options B:

Earrings £20

Necklace £35

Necklace and earrings £35

According to researchers, when consumers are presented with set of options A, the majority will choose the cheaper option of Earrings for £20. However, when given set of options B, customers are more likely to choose the third option (Necklace and earrings £35) when the decoy (Necklace £35) is added as a choice. No consumer will choose just the necklace, when they can essentially get a free pair of earrings. Other buyers may think that for just an extra £15 they can get a necklace worth £35. A smaller percentage of people (who are either more rational or restricted by a budget,) will choose to buy just the earrings.

So, if you want to encourage people to choose a piece of jewellery with higher karats, to sell more bundles of related products, or increase the number of people who add gift packaging to their order, then start using the decoy effect.

Discriminatory Pricing

If you are planning to sell via more than one sales channel, you might wish to use a discriminatory pricing strategy and charge different prices for the same product. With this method, even if you run a shop in a low-income area, you can still sell at higher prices elsewhere. Understandably though, this approach could be considered unfair, especially by customers who discover that they have missed out on a lower price. To avoid any issues, you should make it clear if a product is available more cheaply via one of your other channels.

Another way that businesses can use discriminatory pricing is by offering a reduced rate to specific groups of people, such as students and pensioners. You should always think strategically before implementing this. Is the aim to make prices more affordable for a particular section of your target market, or to lure customers away from the competition? There is no point offering a discount for the sake of it, and it can be difficult to reverse discriminatory pricing once you've started. If you can achieve the same aim using an alternative method, then try that first.

Psychological Pricing

For many years, retailers have used psychological pricing tactics, (such as selling something at £9.99 instead of £10,) to convince buyers that a product is less expensive. Generally this works, although increasingly consumers are becoming aware of such tactics. In fact, some recent studies suggest that rounding up prices may actually work better. Find out which tactic works best for your business.

Price Setting

Ideally, setting a price for a product should not be a one-off event, but rather the first step in an ongoing process that regularly reviews the effect a price has on sales volume and profit. This should reduce the pressure of needing to get it right first time, but you'll still need to come up with a reasonable price to start selling.

So where do you start? Do you base a price purely on mathematical calculations that guarantee a good profit margin and ignore the market price? Do you base it solely on what your customers are willing to pay and risk not making much profit? And what will happen to the price when you have a sale?

The systematic approach discussed below takes into account all the important factors (your profit, your customers, and the market), and solves the problem business owners often have of not knowing where to start.

Figure 6.1 Price Data Gathering Form

	Product A	Product B
1. True unit cost	£________	£________
2. Your Bottom line	£________	£________
3. RRP	£________	£________
4. Competitors' price	£________	£________
5. Minimum customers will pay	£________	£________
6. Maximum customers will pay	£________	£________
Your Price Range	£________ to £________	£________ to £________

1. Calculate the true unit cost

You'll need to calculate the true unit cost, or the break-even price, of each product:

Variable Costs

(The amount your supplier charges per piece including delivery, VAT, import duty, etc)

+

Fixed Costs

(Fixed costs such as rent & rates, utilities, labour, marketing, depreciation of fixed assets, and any other costs that are not affected by sales volume. To calculate these, you should add all your overheads together and then divide by the number of units you expect to sell.)

2. Calculate your bottom line (Cost-plus pricing)

You should decide what profit you want to make on each product. By adding your profit to the true unit cost you can come up with your bottom line, or the lowest price you are willing to sell each product for. In the past, businesses have used various methods for determining their profit margins, including doubling or tripling the original cost. Ultimately, only you can decide what is a worthwhile margin that will enable you to reach your revenue targets.

If you plan to run discount schemes and other margin-reducing promotions, then you need to include this 'cost' in the selling price, or exclude sale items from any discount offers.

3. Supplier prices

Some suppliers provide an RRP (Recommended Retail Price,) or MRSP (Manufacturer's Suggested Retail Price,) as a way of ensuring high profits for themselves and avoiding a price war amongst the retailers that they supply.

However, recommended prices are just that; recommended. In the UK, it is illegal to enforce a minimum or maximum selling price on retailers. Furthermore, while some RRPs may be based on proven sales (i.e., the supplier or a reseller that they supply has sold to consumers at that price,) frequently these inflated figures are invented to make their products seem more appealing to retailers. Therefore, the prices suggested by suppliers should be viewed merely as another source of information to assist you in setting a price of your own choosing, and in some cases you should disregard this source altogether.

4. Competitors' prices

The price your competitors charge for the same or a similar product can be used as a benchmark, provided the companies that you use are similar to yours, e.g., in a similar location with the same target market. Before you take a competitor's prices at face value though, you should research exactly what their offer is. They may have low prices, but charge the earth for postage. Or a product of theirs may have a top price, but they may be yet to sell their first piece. Be sure to take into account any regional price differences, too.

Compare how both you and your competitors add value. Whose offer is the most attractive to customers? What extra benefits and features do you provide? If your competitors do anything better than you, then it may be wise to pitch your prices a little lower than theirs.

5. Minimum customers are willing to pay

Business owners rarely consider the notion that a customer has a minimum price in mind. A minimum price is usually based on a customer's personal beliefs about how much they need to spend on a product for it to be of a satisfactory or desired quality. You can identify this price in your market research, by asking your sample what is the least they would expect to pay for the product.

6. Maximum customers are willing to pay

The maximum price your target market will pay for a product is down to their income and other factors, such as how often they expect to wear the product and how unique it is. You can identify this price in your market research by finding out how much people are willing to spend.

Establishing a Price Range

Once you have filled in the table (Figure 6.1), you can look at the data to establish a price range for your products. The key data you need to compare are prices 2-6, with the most important figures being your bottom line and the price your target market is prepared to pay. The true unit cost only becomes important in situations where you need to sell off stock quickly, (in times of low demand or closure, for example,) as it tells you the lowest price that you should charge so that you can at least break-even.

The Rules for establishing a price range:

1. Your price range should always be within the range that customers are prepared to pay.
2. The lower price of your range should not be lower than your bottom line.
3. You should use RRP's and your competitor's prices as a guide only.

Figure 6.2 shows an example of a completed table with price ranges, along with explanations.

Identifying a price range rather than a single price gives you the flexibility to adjust the price up or down whenever you need to without pricing out customers or making a loss. It also immediately flags up any products that you should discontinue (or avoid stocking in the first place) if the profit they contribute is poor.

Figure 6.2 Example of Price Range Setting

	Product A	Product B	Product C
1. True unit cost	£0.87	£5.00	£11.50
2. Your Bottom line	£2.25	£10.50	£16.99
3. RRP	£3.99	n/a	£14.00
4. Competitors price	£3.99	£15.00	£14.95
5. Min customers will pay	£3.00	£10.00	£10.00
6. Max customers will pay	£4.50	£12.00	£15.00
Your Price Range	**£2.25 - £4.50**	**£10.50 - £12.00**	**-**

Product A – In an ideal world, your bottom line would be the lowest price, and the maximum that customers are willing to pay would be the highest, with the RRP and competitor's prices confirming that you are in the right range.

Product B – Many competitors will pitch their prices at the RRP if suppliers provide them, but if a competitor is successfully selling at a higher price, then it suggests that it may be possible to sell at above the recommended price too. It is, however, the customer's budget that will ultimately determine the upper price of your range.

Product C – The bottom line is higher than the maximum that customers will pay, and the RRP and competitors prices are lower than your bottom line. Unless you take a hit on your profit margin, Product C will not sell enough units at a good profit and so should be avoided.

Setting a Starting Price

Setting a price is relatively easy if you have a narrow price range to work with. In fact, a price range could be so small that the only decision you have to make is a minor tactical one, such as whether to charge £10.99 or £11.00. If you have a much wider scope, it is easy to become overwhelmed trying to decide whether to launch with a price at the upper, middle, or lower end of its range. The price you choose will depend largely on your pricing strategy and revenue targets. However, it is not necessarily the launch price that is important…

The Art of Pricing: Making Adjustments

The real art of pricing is not in the setting of a price, but in the evaluations and adjustments that you make to that price in the weeks, months, and even years that follow.

Finding the Optimum Price

Businesses rarely get a price right first time, so once you have a price range to work with, it is down to trial and error to find the price that contributes the most revenue.

Generally, lowering prices increases sales volume and lowers your profit margin, while raising prices tends to decrease sales volume but increase your profit margin.

You should avoid making any substantial changes, and instead make gradual adjustments and monitor the effect on sales volume and revenue. These adjustments should be within your identified price range; never lower than your bottom line; never higher than what the customer is willing to pay; and always at a level that provides a good profit. At the same time you need to protect your brand image, and keep an eye on competitors in case they respond with their own price changes.

The continuous process

As well as tweaking your prices in the weeks and months following a product's launch, you'll need to make adjustments in response to economic and social changes. The jewellery and accessories market, and retail in general, is never static and is therefore vulnerable to external factors such as economic fluctuations, inflation, fashion trends, changes in exchange rates, suppliers going bust, competitors leaving and entering the market, and new laws.

Business owners may be reluctant to make price changes (particularly increases) in case customers go elsewhere. But success in the long term is all about getting the psychology right, by managing a product's perceived value, and making small price changes rather than obvious price hikes.

The timing also must be right. If you know that milder spring weather is on its way for example, you can push for some last minute sales of scarves, gloves and leg wear by lowering their prices. At Christmas, harassed shoppers care less about the ticket price and so you can normally raise prices without a problem.

Developing an instinct

Many entrepreneurs develop a good instinct for setting prices when they have been trading for a few years and have gained industry experience. So, once your business is established, and as long as you know the unit costs of the products you are selling, it may not be necessary to follow the price range system quite so meticulously or adjust your selling prices as many times.

In the next chapter, we will look at how to attract customers to your business with the right advertising, and how to make the most of the free publicity methods that are available.

7

Attracting Customers

Everything so far has been geared towards creating the perfect proposition for your target market; from sourcing the products that they want to buy and setting the right prices, to choosing the best sales channels and designing a brand concept that gives your products desirability. All that is left to do is raise awareness of your business and get customers through your doors.

A clear strategy, and an understanding of your target market, is vital if you want to avoid wasting time and money on advertising that is ineffective and inappropriate for your business. Some of the most effective publicity methods are actually free to implement, so it makes sense to utilise these as much as possible.

Attracting customers successfully is about discovering which methods work best for your business. This is achieved through setting goals for your campaigns, and then making correct evaluations.

Advertising & Publicity Options

Advertising and publicity are actually two different things. Advertising is usually paid-for marketing over a specified period of time or set number of occasions, such as a classified ad that appears on a website for one month. In contrast, publicity often requires a lot of creativity but generally very little money to put into action.

As you will see from the list below, there is a wide choice of marketing options that you can use to get your message across to potential customers.

Advertising

- Newspapers & magazines
- Flyers and leaflets
- Brochures
- Posters
- Newspaper inserts
- Classified advertisements
- Directories
- Email marketing
- Pay Per Click advertising
- TV advertising
- Radio advertising
- Online video advertising
- SMS text messaging
- Telemarketing
- Billboards & sign picketing

Publicity

- Media coverage
- Shows and events
- Seminars and talks
- Promotional giveaways
- Event sponsorship
- Press releases
- Networking
- Company website
- Window displays
- Corporate videos & tutorials
- Podcasts and vlogs
- Competitions
- Social network presence
- Newsletters & blogs
- Publicity stunts

Choosing the right options

In an ideal world it would be great to use every possible marketing option from the above list to maximise the number of people that your marketing campaign will reach. However, there is no point wasting time on methods that won't enable you to connect with your target market or provide a good return on your investment. By researching the pros and cons of each marketing option, you'll be able to choose the most effective ways to attract new customers to your business.

The permanence offered by a marketing option could be one factor to compare. Setting up a page on Facebook for example, can have a lasting impact, as once it is created the page will always exist on the internet. Moreover, with regular updates, more users can become fans of your business and the effect can snowball. In contrast, an advertisement in a weekly newspaper has a temporary effect, and will probably only generate sales during that particular week.

Another aspect to consider is the level of engagement it offers. Social media is all about interaction, but a radio advert is one-sided, with no chance for customers to be involved other than to listen.

Even if a marketing option is free, you'll need to consider the reputations of the 'locations' and advertising organisations with whom you align yourself, as you don't want your business to be associated with any negative or unsuitable publicity. A billboard next to a gentleman's club may not be the image you want to project to potential customers. You can also see how important it is to manage your business links and take action when needed, from the speed at which companies pull out of sponsorship deals with disgraced celebrities.

Reaching your Target Market

Your research findings should offer guidance on the best approaches to promote your business. If you know which magazines and websites your target market like, you could think about advertising in these, or if you know that prospects like to visit jewellery shows, you could consider exhibiting or giving a talk at the events they attend.

You should also get into the habit of asking existing customers how they found your business, to give you an idea of the best way to attract similar customers in the future.

Possibly the most important thing to consider is the number of potential customers you will reach using a specific advertiser or medium.

If you plan to advertise in a magazine or newspaper, then find out how many people read the publication (you can check the ABC circulation figures) and their readership demographics (most advertisers will provide this information for you.) If you plan to advertise on websites, you can use Alexa.com for free to find out the site's ranking, traffic sources, and audience statistics, before you invest.

There are many factors that can affect the success of advertising and publicity, but sometimes you have to take a risk. It can be difficult to predict the effectiveness of publicity methods such as flash mobbing, especially if it is something that has never been done before in your area.

Attracting Customers on a Budget

The cost of marketing options can range from the very expensive (such as television advertising) to the free (such as writing a press release.) Your budget will ultimately dictate what you can and can't do to attract customers to your business. Fortunately, there are plenty of ways to achieve your aims without the need for an enormous marketing budget.

Organise an Event

By organising a pre-loved or vintage sale, a jewellery design career day, or a regular coffee morning, you will attract new people to your shop and increase your revenue. Even if people don't buy anything during these events, your brand name will be at the forefront of their minds when they need to buy jewellery and accessories, and they will be more likely to recommend you to their friends.

You should think about how you can use your professional skills and knowledge to create exciting events for people. If you make jewellery and accessories, and you think you could teach others, then you could run a regular class and charge a fee. Even if you don't have any relevant skills or knowledge yourself, then you could invite guest speakers instead.

Referral Schemes

If you have been trading for a little while, you could try to increase your customer base with a Recommend a Friend scheme, whereby you offer a small incentive, usually a discount, to get your current customers to give you their friend's details (with their friend's permission, of course.) It's good practice to offer an incentive to both your customer and their friend, as it will help you to obtain the referral from your existing customer and also persuade the new customer to make a purchase.

Social Networking

Using social networking sites such as Facebook is a great way to raise awareness of your business. In your primary and secondary research you should have identified whether your target market uses these sites, and therefore whether it would be worth setting up social media pages for your own business. Even if your target market aren't prolific users of social networks, having a social presence can still help to attract customers by increasing the chances of them finding you. Having an *active* social presence can help reassure customers that you are currently trading and haven't closed down.

Once up and running, you can start by asking your friends and family to become fans of your page, and then ask them to spread the word. To speed up the process, you could launch a customer photo competition or run a post of the month contest. You can also poach fans from your rivals, by sending friend requests to the followers of other jewellery and accessories businesses.

Many campaigns to increase followers can quickly snowball when people see their friends becoming fans. With a little effort, you can gain a pool of potential customers to whom you can promote your business, in a relatively short space of time.

Offer a chance to win a Money-Can't-Buy Prize

People love winning things, so why not launch a competition to get the public designing a new accessory or piece of jewellery. The winner could get their design produced and stocked by your company.

If you sell coveted designer pieces, offering one in a prize draw can attract a large number of new sign-ups and customers. When the prizes have a high value, you'll want to ensure you get a good return on your investment by planning a timely campaign. You should be able to gain good media coverage by leveraging the support of industry journalists and bloggers, and using social networking.

Publicity Stunts

One of the most bizarre things done to garner publicity for Prince & Princess Petwear was to create a dog collar with a built-in Rolex watch. It's a ridiculous, crazy concept; exactly the sort of story that the tabloids love. The Sun and The Daily Mail both ran the piece. Within hours, "The Watchdog" was being discussed on news sites and blogs all around the world. 'Prince & Princess Petwear' was Googled thousands of times by people checking to see if the story was actually true. Most importantly, traffic to the website, and sales, went through the roof.

Multinational companies pay huge sums for that amount of world-wide coverage, and we got it for free just for coming up with a tabloid-friendly story. By thinking outside the box, you too can come up with marketing stunts that will get people talking.

In another example, a £12000 diamond was dropped from the edge of space for The Diamond in the Sky stunt in 2014, which sparked a four-month treasure hunt by members of the public. The stunt was created by Shackleton PR for online retailer 77 Diamonds. It's not essential to hire an expensive PR firm though, as brainstorming ideas with staff, friends and customers can often be equally productive.

News Stories

Of course, you don't have to churn out wacky ideas each time in order to get free publicity. If you are able to build a good relationship with your local newspaper, by providing them with newsworthy stories, it should guarantee regular publicity for your business. Possible stories could cover anniversaries, product launches, the winning of an award, the 1000th customer through your door, free giveaways for readers, charity fundraising, record attempts, and exposés of the jewellery trade. If you have such a story, write a good press release and send it to the paper in the body of an email. Don't give up if your first story isn't used by a particular publication. Instead, try a different publication or come up with a different story idea. It can take several attempts, but the media coverage is always worth it.

The Magic word

FREE! Nothing grabs people's attention like the word 'free'. Everyone likes getting something for nothing, especially if it is something of value to them. Think about what you can give to your customers that can be valuable to them. Free style advice guides, promo gifts, or prize draws entries can be offered in exchange for getting a prospect's details, which you can then use for future marketing campaigns.

Your Website: The Ultimate Advert

Whichever marketing options you choose, a web presence is a must for any business trading in the 21st Century. Whether you run a basic informational webpage or a full-blown ecommerce shop, a website is the ultimate advertisement, doing its job 24 hours a day, 365 days a year. Your site, therefore, needs to follow the rules of a good advert by ensuring each page is attractive and gets its message across, whether that be 'call us today', 'buy now' or 'sign up here'.

A website can provide a lot more information than the average advertisement, but as a bare minimum it should include details of who you are, what you do, your contact details, why you started up, and your mission statement. Of course, none of this will matter if no one is able to find your site...

Increasing Your Website's Visibility

There is no point in investing lots of money and time in building a website if few people get to see it, which is why you need to be proactive in generating visitors, or 'traffic'. The traffic to your website can come from the following sources:

Direct - People who reach your website by typing in your ULR (or web address), by clicking on a link in an email, or via a bookmark they have created, all form 'direct traffic.' You can increase direct visitors by having your web address in as many places as possible, including on all of your marketing materials, vehicles, signage, staff uniforms, and your email signature. In addition, using a QR (Quick Response) code wherever possible, as well as your written web address, may further increase direct traffic.

Referrals – These come from links from other sites on the internet. You can increase links by adding your website's details to related online directories (start with ISEdb.com, which is a directory of directories, and work your way through the shopping, jewellery and fashion sites). Not only will these back links send traffic straight to your website, they will convince search engines such as Google that your website is popular and deserves a top ranking. Don't build too many links at once, (four or five per week at most), as Google will pick up on this and it will count against you.

Links from your blog, social media, and article submissions can refer high volumes of traffic to your website. However, banner ads, (another type of referral,) tend to be unpopular with internet users.

Search engines – The majority of visitors will arrive at a website through one of the big search engines such as Google, Yahoo, Ask, Bing, or Dogpile. A large number of people searching don't scroll down the first page of results, even less click onto the second page. Therefore, if your website doesn't rank near the top, then to the vast majority of people you simply won't exist.

There are two ways to achieve a top ranking in the SERPS; paid-for advertising, which yields short-term results; and free organic search engine optimisation, which should eventually generate around 75% of the total traffic to your site.

Pay Per Click Advertising

You can instantly get to the top of SERPs with Pay Per Click (PPC) advertising from providers such as Google AdWords and Yahoo! Search Marketing, as long as you are willing to bid high enough per click.

Many businesses believe that the aim of their Pay Per Click ad campaigns is to achieve a number one position. However, when a potential customer searches online for an item, they rarely buy from the first result that Google provides. More typically, once a customer has looked at the first ranked website, they will return to the results page and check the second and third ranked sites. If all websites are offering similar products at similar prices, will they then return to the first website to buy? Many remain on the website that they are currently viewing and make a purchase or an enquiry. Therefore, you'll probably have much more success aiming for the rankings just below the top spot, and the PPC rates will be cheaper.

Generating the right keywords is an important part of PPC advertising. You will need to think about the products that you are selling, and the key phrases people use to search for them. Google's Keyword Tool is invaluable, as it shows you the number of searches per month and the level of competition for keywords. You can also see what keywords a competitor's website is targeting. Specificity is key. 'Women's sunglasses' may be too broad a term. 'Women's Aviator sunglasses' may narrow the results down, but you'll still have a high level of competition. 'Women's Ray-Ban aviator sunglasses' may be relevant enough to get you a good SERPs position.

Search Engine Optimisation

Quite possibly, your biggest online PPC expenditure will occur in the weeks and months after your launch, as you try to increase traffic and generate sales. However, once people start to find your website naturally in the results pages, you should be able to reduce your online advertising budget. You'll only need to raise it again when you need to boost sales during quiet or highly competitive periods, or you are running a specific campaign.

Achieving a high-ranking by organic means takes time, but you can make it happen by:

- Providing the best web experience, with clear navigation and fast page loading
- Having a website design that is responsive to different browsers and devices
- Considering how the page title and meta description tags display to search engine users
- Including relevant H1 Headers on pages
- Ensuring that written content is relevant to target market search queries
- Avoiding duplicate content by writing unique product descriptions
- Using relevant keywords within proper sentences on pages but avoiding keyword stuffing
- Regularly updating your site by adding new content (e.g., a blog)
- Ensuring all of your images have ALT tags, which include your primary keyword
- Improving your link popularity
- Adding a sitemap
- Improving your reputation with likes, tweets, and shares by adding social sharing buttons
- Using a domain name that includes relevant keywords
- Having short and well-organised URLs for every page
- Linking to some credible external websites that may be relevant to your target market

If all of this sounds like your worst nightmare, then it is probably a good idea to hire someone to optimise your site for you. Nevertheless, since SEO is an ongoing process, if you can learn to do some of these things yourself, then you can save yourself a lot of money.

Recruiting Existing Customers

If you have an established business, you can recruit your existing customers to help you increase your customer base.

Reviews

One medium that is highly popular is online reviews sites such as Reviewcentre.com, where customers can rate products and services. You can encourage your existing customers to post reviews about your business, which will encourage new people to find out more about you and boost your profile. For online businesses, it's a good idea to enable a customer review facility on the product pages, as it can eliminate any pre-purchase doubts your visitors may have during the buying process. Don't be afraid of getting bad reviews either; they help to make the positive reviews more believable.

If any of your customers write a popular blog or have lots of followers on social network sites, consider sending them some sample products to test, and encourage them to post their thoughts to their friends and followers.

Word of Mouth

Word of mouth advertising occurs when people tell their friends, family, work colleagues, and neighbours about their experience with a particular business or product. Unfortunately, most people tend to talk about a company only after they've had a bad experience. For customers to speak positively and make recommendations about you, it usually takes *something exceptional.*

Many business owners mistakenly believe that word of mouth advertising is something that they cannot influence. While it is impossible to control what your customers say to others, you can create the WOW factor, that *something exceptional* that will make customers want to tell their friends about you. In Chapter 8, we look in-depth at how to create exceptional customer service and get customers to spread the word on your behalf.

Setting Goals & Evaluating

Whether you want to increase sales, increase your customer base, raise awareness of your business, or simply get more people to sign up to your newsletter, you should have clear aims about what you want to gain from the marketing options you select. Setting goals will enable you to review your marketing effort at regular intervals, and make any necessary improvements, or even cease a campaign if it is not accomplishing what you hoped it would.

Having the ability to track and monitor the results of your marketing is important if you want to find out what works and what does not. Monitoring your campaigns is much easier if you use a unique promotional code in each of your adverts, and ask customers to quote this when they get in touch. Google Analytics and WebTrends are great for tracking the response of campaigns, but if you use paper vouchers you will have to deal with these codes manually in order to calculate the response rate.

If you get a good response from an ad campaign, (such as a clear increase in visitors to your boutique,) but you don't achieve your primary goal of increased sales, then you will need to review your website, premises, and staff, to find out what is putting off potential customers.

If you don't get increased enquiries, orders or click-throughs from a campaign, then it is the adverts themselves that are ineffective and you should re-examine the imagery, copy and language used, as well as the media in which you have placed your adverts.

The problem could be caused by an inconsistency between your advert and your business. When creating advertising content, we all want to present our businesses in the best possible light, but sometimes we may stretch the truth a little too much. You could, for example, have a stunning advert that gives the impression that your business carries a huge range when it doesn't. Or a flyer that suggests your jewellery and accessories are mid-priced brands when your store is a high-end luxury boutique. It is easy for customers to feel disappointed and deceived when they realise that a proposition has not been reflected accurately. Your advertising and publicity must match your brand and reflect your offer, otherwise it will be easy to attract prospects, but hard to convert them into paying customers.

In the next chapter, we shall discuss how to keep the customers you have attracted, through good communication, rewards and exceptional customer service.

Keeping Customers

I t costs much less to retain existing customers than it does to attract new ones. Nevertheless, you would be surprised how many businesses spend time and money acquiring customers, only to neglect them in the pursuit of attracting more new customers.

Just because a customer has bought from you in the past, it doesn't mean that they are loyal or that they will even remember you the next time they need to buy jewellery and accessories. Most customers need some sort of regular reminder that you exist.

Keeping customers interested in your business is much easier when you have their contact details. Although you do need to be mindful because no one likes being bombarded with unwanted marketing.

Once you have earned a customer's loyalty you will need to reward them in order to retain them in the long-term. As we will discover, rewards do not have to break the bank for them to be effective.

Retaining Customers

Proactively retaining customers is something that all businesses must do to generate a steady income. There are three things you should do to retain customers:

1. Be customer focused;
2. Communicate regularly;
3. Reward loyalty.

1. Be Customer Focused

A business that puts the customer at the centre of its operation will make customers feel valued and encourage repeat sales.

New Products, Services, and Events

One way you can retain customers is by meeting their changing needs with new products and services. Not only does this show your customers that their needs are important to you, it also makes them want to return regularly to find out what new products they can buy.

Events such as coffee mornings and jewellery-making classes, are a good excuse to get your customers to come back, and it demonstrates to them that you are more than just a retailer trying to make a profit.

Seek Customer Suggestions

By seeking the opinions of your existing customers, you can garner information about how to improve and grow your business, and you will demonstrate to your customers that you are putting them at the heart of everything that you do.

Exceptional Customer Service

You need to give customers a reason to buy from you rather than the competition. More often than not, your biggest opportunity to compete (especially with the big players) will lie in your customer service. If you can identify your competitors' weaknesses in this area, and then offer a superior service, you should be able to get customers coming back to you.

There are many ways to create exceptional customer service including:

- Providing helpful, honest, and highly-knowledgeable sales assistance
- Treating the customer as an individual
- Caring for the customer by being courteous and attentive (think 'personal shopper' whenever you deal with them)
- Engaging with customers and creating a rapport with them
- Providing quality at every step of the buying process (including after-sales)
- Putting the customer at the centre of everything you do (e.g. when designing new products)
- Keeping your promises

Complaint Handling

At some point, you will encounter a complaint from a customer. It could be because they were sold an item with a defect or sent the wrong colour or size. Sometimes, it won't even be due to a failure on your part.

The great thing about receiving a complaint is that it is a chance to prove to the customer that you are professional and honest. After all, until something goes wrong, customers won't really know if they can trust you. If you are able to listen, and focus on a satisfactory solution to the problem, you can win a customer's lifetime loyalty.

It is worth mentioning here that not all customers are worth keeping. Some customers are a drain on your resources and bring in little revenue in return. Don't be afraid to let customers go if they persistently cause you problems and are hard to please. You can cease marketing communications to these individuals, or even politely explain that you don't think your business has anything to offer them. Then you can focus your energy on your other customers or on finding new ones.

2. Communicate Regularly

It can seem a little unfair that customers who have had a positive experience with your business quickly forget, while those who have encountered a problem seem to remember forever. Regular communication is the key to ensuring that the customers who love what you do are reminded to buy from you again.

Permission Marketing

Before sending emails, mailings, or any other marketing communications to prospects, you will need to obtain their permission. Rather than this being something that restricts you though, it makes your marketing effort more effective because you focus only on the people who are most receptive to what you have to say. Collecting and organising data is time consuming, so you'll want your database to contain only quality leads. This ensures that you're not wasting time on people who ignore your communications, or worse, are infuriated by them.

There are a number of ways you can obtain permission to contact customers. You could invite customers to sign up to your newsletter, or request their details in exchange for a prize draw entry or discount code. If you run an online shop, then a checkbox to opt-in or opt-out (to your marketing offers and news) during the checkout process can have a high success rate.

Obtaining consent is just one part of your task. Seth Godin, the author and marketing guru, said that permission marketing was a privilege given to businesses by customers, to deliver *relevant* communications. In other words, if a customer is only interested in costume jewellery, then don't waste their time by sending them details of your fine jewellery range.

If you are unable to create a different version of an email or mail shot for each of your target groups (usually based on the customer's product interests or price points), then a general campaign that has something for everyone is the next best thing.

Whether you are able to send targeted communications or not, you must make sure that you only contact prospects when you have something of value to say. Sending out a monthly marketing email because it is 'just something you do' is not a good enough reason for spamming somebody's inbox. At best, your recipients will start to delete your emails without reading then. At worst, they will request that you remove their details from your mailing list and you will have lost a potentially good contact. A new product line, a clearance sale, or a discount voucher, are good examples of what might be valuable to your customers.

You need to protect your customer's data by keeping it secure, and only using it for the purposes for which they have agreed. Some organisations sell their marketing data to third parties, but buyers and sellers of this data forget that the most valuable aspect, the *permission* given by customers, cannot be transferred. Having permission will give you an edge over any competitors using bought mailing lists, and ultimately you'll generate more repeat sales. So, even if you have the consent to sell the data to third parties, don't.

Marketing Methods

You can use the same marketing options listed in Chapter 7 to retain customers as well as attract them. However, some methods such as newspaper advertising can be expensive, and are not always a cost-effective way of keeping your existing customers updated. If you have your customer's permission to use their email address, postal address, or phone number, or they are following you on Facebook, then it makes sense to market directly to them using these methods.

Email Marketing

Email is an easy and effective way to keep in contact with your customers and anyone that has subscribed to your marketing updates. And, best of all, it is free.

You can send plain text emails to your mailing list, although the success rate tends to be higher if you send the more professional-looking newsletter-style (HTML) emails via an e-marketing company such as Constant Contact or Mail Chimp. These software providers make it relatively simple to create different email campaigns for your different customer groups, too.

It can be all too easy to overuse this method, largely because it is free, but also because it allows you to communicate with an infinite number of people with just the click of the send button.

One obstacle to the effectiveness of email marketing is getting your message to stand out amongst the many other communications that your contacts receive throughout the day. Using catchy headlines and personalising emails with the recipient's name can improve your success rate. It may help to note any emails you receive that grab your attention, and ask yourself what they did that worked. You can then use the same techniques when creating your own campaigns.

Mailshots

You can keep in touch with customers by sending out mailshots such as letters, leaflets, brochures, postcards, and invitations.

Mailshots are a good way to reach certain customer groups, including the older generation that perhaps don't respond as well to electronic methods of marketing. If your competitors are relying solely on modern media to promote their business, then it might be worth sending your customers a mailshot instead, just to have a better chance of getting noticed.

The increasing printing and postage costs, as well as design charges, can make this an expensive option though, even when economies of scale apply (the more mailings you send out, the cheaper each one will be.) There is also the environmental impact to consider. Some customers are conscious of the cost to the planet and might think less favourably if you start sending them stuff in the post. You should find out how they feel about receiving mailshots when you conduct your primary research.

Telephone Calls

Telephoning customers to keep them updated is a way to guarantee that they personally receive your message, whether it is an invitation to an event, an update on the items they have been waiting for, or just a friendly hello. The fact that you have taken the time to call them will make them feel valued, and you could use the opportunity to do a bit of market research, too.

There can be disadvantages though. If you have a large contact list, it could take a long time to call everyone, and your phone bill could skyrocket if some of your contacts are in a chatty mood when you ring. In contrast, calling at an inconvenient time can be detrimental to your campaign. If you decide to use this method, it is probably best to reserve it for your best and most familiar customers. Being on familiar terms with your contacts means that you will know exactly how to greet each individual, and whether to take an informal or formal tone. Knowing this will help you to get the most out of every call.

SMS Text Messaging

Unlike email, most people will read a text before they delete it. While you don't have as many characters in which to stimulate an emotional response and trigger a call to action, busy people who are bombarded by marketing communications will definitely appreciate such brevity.

The increasing numbers of smartphones is great news for businesses that choose to market by SMS, and it means you can stimulate an immediate response from your recipients, such as getting them to phone you or to visit your website via a link.

Obviously, you could send individual texts from a mobile phone handset, but if you are sending a lot of messages it will be more cost- and time-effective to use a text message provider, such as Text Marketer. Another benefit is that it is much easier to target the specific customer groups on your mailing list.

Social Networking

Making use of social networking sites, such as Facebook and Twitter, is different from other marketing methods. For a start, you don't need to obtain any personal contact details; you just need to get people to follow you. This tends to be an easier task if you have an existing online presence, because you can encourage people to click through to your social pages via links on your website, product listings, or business profile.

Social networking sites are free to use, but you will need to update your followers regularly in order to keep them engaged. To be effective, your updates should encourage two-way communication as much as possible. This can be achieved in various ways, including by posing market research questions, setting up polls, starting debates, or simply chatting with your followers.

If you have a big following, social networking can enable you to launch events such as clearance sales, at very short notice because word will quickly spread. The major downside to social networking is that you cannot target specific groups with tailored messages, so your updates need to appeal to all followers.

Public Relations

Public Relations, or PR, concerns all your business communications with the public and includes emails to customers, letters, advertisements, your website, blog and any articles written about you in the media. Good PR can help give you and your business credibility, build awareness of your brand, and present your business in the best possible light.

PR really comes into its own when things go wrong, such as in the event of a product recall. If managed correctly, PR can help avert a crisis, limit damage to your brand's image, and ensure that both potential and existing customers are not discouraged from buying from you in the future.

PR is an entire discipline, with many books and training courses available on the subject, but you can see how professional PR spokespeople do it by watching the news or consumer affairs programmes.

3. Rewards

We all know how it feels when a company that we have been loyal to entices new customers with great discounts and free gifts, whilst overlooking its existing customers. By rewarding all customers equally, they will reward you with their loyalty.

Gold Card

Loyalty schemes are an effective way to encourage customers to keep returning. You could offer reward points every time people shop with you, and they could earn gifts or money-off vouchers when they've collected enough points. If customers are working towards a 'prize' from your business, they won't want to spend their money with your competitors.

You might also want to give your very best customers membership of a VIP club, and then offer them privileges such as discount vouchers, special events, and free delivery. Customers that feel they are part of a special group are much more likely to stay loyal to your business.

Treat Customers like Friends

There are some simple and inexpensive ways to show customers that you are thinking of them.

If you get a customer buying jewellery for her engagement party for example, then giving her a courtesy call just to find out how it all went will make her more likely to return in the future. Similarly, your male customers will be forever grateful if you send them a timely reminder of their partner's or mother's upcoming birthday, and offer them advice on choosing the perfect present.

Sending birthday and Christmas cards to customers in the post used to be a ubiquitous exercise, but since many companies now send emails instead, returning to tradition might help your business stand out. It can certainly make customers feel as though they are part of the 'family,' and they will be impressed that you remembered them.

The Power of Free

As discussed in Chapter 7, giving something away for nothing, such as a promotional gift or a written guide, is a great incentive to get people through your doors and make a purchase. Existing customers respond equally well to receiving free stuff, and the promise of future freebies in exchange for repeat purchases can keep your customers loyal.

Enlist your Customers' Help

Everyone likes to feel needed. If you can get customers to help you, even in a small way such as by recommending you to their friends, liking you on Facebook, or suggesting ways to improve, then they will feel that they are an integral part of your business.

As stated previously, you could involve your customers by launching a competition to design a product, or include them in buying decisions by getting them to vote for brands they'd like you to stock.

You don't have to give away gifts and discounts to show your appreciation either. Simply saying thank you to customers for their support can be enough of a reward.

If you have a customer that really loves what you do, then consider hiring them. Even if you are unable to offer them a full-time job, you could take advantage of their enthusiasm by getting them to host home parties, or hiring them to help you sell at events.

Give them a mention

Some customers love to hear their name given a mention and there are probably plenty of opportunities within your business to do this. You could set up a photo gallery on your website, mention a competition winner's name in your blog or newsletter, or have a notice board with customer photos and messages in your boutique. On social media, the act of sharing a customer's post can be an effective way to acknowledge followers, albeit in a more low-key way.

In the next chapter, we shall discover how you can use your financial records to make better business decisions, and how to troubleshoot financial problems when they arise.

⑨

Improving Your Financial Performance

Keeping accurate financial records is more than just a legal requirement. Your books, profit and loss account, and balance sheet provide the only true indicator of your business's well-being; its profitability.

Unfortunately, these documents can only tell you what has happened in the past, when it may be too late to rectify any serious issues. By collecting just a few additional statistics and organising the data, you can uncover a mine of information that is hiding in your financial books. Furthermore, if any problems do begin to arise, you'll be able to immediately pinpoint the source (income, outgoings, or cash flow) and implement the correct solutions. Keeping these additional records doesn't have to take up a lot of extra time. Accounting programs or spreadsheets such as Excel, will do most of the work.

Keeping Records

Single or Double Entry Books?

Given the limited time that business owners have, it is understandable that many maintain just the bare minimum of financial records. Keeping basic, single-entry books will satisfy the taxman, but they won't really tell you much apart from what you earned and spent in a particular period.

Double-entry bookkeeping presents a breakdown of your incomings and outgoings, so you can see exactly how each area of your business is performing.

Figure 9.1 Example of Purchases Book

Date	Details	Total	Ref	Stock	Rent	Legal	P+P
2.3.12	Mail Service	£9.67	001				£9.67
3.3.12	Supplier X	£76.00	002	£76.00			
3.3.12	AB Insurance	£8.00	003			£8.00	
4.3.12	Mail Service	£4.55	004				£4.55

Figure 9.2 Example: Sales Book

Date	Details	Total	Ref	Website	Parties	Shop
1.3.12	Wilkins, T.	£45.50	001	£45.50		
2.3.12	Clark, P	£23.99	002			£23.99
2.3.12	Johnson, S	£15.00	003	£15.00		
5.3.12	Ball, M	£160.00	004		£160.00	

Keeping Up To Date Books

Some proprietors are so busy with the day-to-day running of their business that they struggle to find the time to maintain up-to-date records. If it's not a tax return deadline that motivates business owners to get organised, then it is the knowledge that avoiding the books for too long can have serious financial repercussions.

Many EPoS systems and ecommerce solutions will record transactions as they occur, but when automation is not possible you'll need to update your books manually, preferably on a daily basis. Leaving your paperwork to pile up for more than a week can make it harder to start the task and longer to complete when you finally get around to it.

By bookkeeping little and often, you will spot the first warning signs of financial problems and be able to take any necessary action at the earliest opportunity. If you have an online sales target of £2500 per month for example, but you only update your books once every fortnight, then it will be the middle of the month when you discover whether or not you are on course to meet that £2500 target. And, if things aren't going well, then you only have two weeks to get back on track.

Management Accounting: Uncovering your Books' Hidden Potential

By applying the current and historical data that you have from your double-entry books, and collecting some additional statistics, you can identify trends and patterns, and use them to make better decisions.

This data can help you to:
- Decide when and how much stock to purchase.
- Monitor the effects of price changes, promotions, marketing, and external factors
- Control your debtors account and expenses
- Improve your stock control
- Compare original forecasts with actual to check that you're on target
- Decide when to pay bills

- Compare profit and expenses with those from previous weeks, months and years, to measure business growth (or decline)
- Identify sales trends to maximise profit
- Identify areas for improvement to achieve your profit goals
- Choose which products to promote and which to discontinue
- Avert financial disaster

Analysing Your Performance

Below are examples of some of the records you can keep to assist you in making better decisions and staying afloat.

How to Check if Your Business is Growing

Gross Profit Margin

> **Gross Profit Margin as a percentage of sales =**
> (Total revenue – Cost of Goods Sold) ÷ Total Revenue x100

The gross profit margin is the difference between your revenue and costs. It can be used to measure the efficiency of your overall sales, individual products, or product ranges. To find the gross profit margin of individual products, you should use the total revenue of each product (*the selling price x the number of units sold*) and the total unit costs of the product sold.

If you want to find out if your efficiency is improving, you'll need to record the gross profit margin over time, and then make comparisons between the months or years.

Net Profit Margin

The net profit margin is another measurement of efficiency, which reveals how well your business converts revenue into real profit after all of your expenses have been calculated.

> **Net Profit Margin =**
>   (Total Revenue – Expenses) ÷ Total Revenue   x100

The net profit margin will tell you the amount of profit you make for every £1 of sales revenue. A percentage of 58%, for example, means that for every £1 of sales you make, 58p is profit. Having a low net profit margin would indicate that your pricing strategies and expenses need to be reviewed. Having a very low net profit could spell disaster if you suffer a decline in sales. To spot such problems in advance, you'll need to record the net profit margin over time, and then make comparisons across the months and years.

How to Control your Expenses

An expenses breakdown will enable you to monitor your individual monthly outgoings. If you keep double-entry books this information can be easily copied and pasted into a spreadsheet and used to help you to pinpoint problems.

Figure 9.3 Example: Expenses Breakdown

	Rent	Phone	Advertising	Travel	Fees	Total
January	£500	£25	£130	£40	£28	£723
February	£500	£29	£150	£56	£44	£779

Multi-Sales Channel Expenses

You can monitor the expenses of each of your sales channels to see which channels are costing you the most to operate:

Figure 9.4 Example: Sales Channels Expenses

	Shop	Website	Home Parties	Auction Sites
January	£300	£100	£40	£56
February	£476	£89	£37	£79

Once you have several months of data you can use it to predict future expenses and manage your cash flow better.

Be careful not to assume that if one of your sales channels has high outgoings, then it must be draining your business and not efficiently generating profit. To get an accurate indication of the performance of your channels, you must compare the net profit margins, as this takes into account both the revenue and the expenses from each channel. Where necessary, apportion any costs that are not produced solely by one single channel, such as the depreciation of a piece of equipment that is shared by all your sales channels.

How to Identify Sales Trends to Maximise Profit

Value and volume of sales

Monitoring the number and value of the sales you make in a given time period, can help you spot patterns and trends. Many businesses analyse sales statistics month by month, but for more in-depth information, you could record it on a weekly, daily, or even hourly basis. Sales data can help determine many things, including the best times to run adverts and promotions, the optimum opening times for your store, the amount of stock and supplies you need to purchase, and the number of staff you'll need to meet expected demand at a given time.

Figure 9.5 Example: Sales Data Records

Hourly

	Total Sales
Hour 1	
Hour 2	
Hour 3	
Hour 4	
Hour 24	

Daily

	Total Sales
Day 1	
Day 2	
Day 3	
Day 4	
Day 31	

<table>
<tr><td colspan="2" align="center">Weekly</td><td></td><td colspan="2" align="center">Monthly</td></tr>
<tr><td></td><td>Total Sales</td><td></td><td></td><td>Total Sales</td></tr>
<tr><td>Week 1</td><td></td><td></td><td>Month 1</td><td></td></tr>
<tr><td>Week 2</td><td></td><td></td><td>Month 2</td><td></td></tr>
<tr><td>Week 3</td><td></td><td></td><td>Month 3</td><td></td></tr>
<tr><td>Week 4</td><td></td><td></td><td>Month 4</td><td></td></tr>
<tr><td>Week 52</td><td></td><td></td><td>Month 12</td><td></td></tr>
</table>

In the 'Total Sales' columns, you could record the total number of sales, the total value of sales, bookings, website page hits, footfall, or any other factors that you think will provide useful information. Once enough data has been gathered, you should be able to see if any patterns emerge.

Individual Product Sales

A breakdown of the sales of each product can help you to decide how much stock you will need at various times of the year.

Figure 9.6 Monthly Sales Record

	Jan	Feb	Mar	Apr	May	Jun	Jul	Aug	Sep	Oct	Nov	Dec
Product A	11	12	6	1	0	0	0	1	9	18	20	23
Product B	18	22	20	21	21	19	20	21	21	22	23	24

In the example above (figure 9.6), 'Product A' sells well during autumn and winter, but not in the summer months. Therefore, you would need to buy enough units by September and sell them all by the spring. 'Product B' seems to be a steady-selling product, and therefore, it should be relatively easy to maintain the appropriate stock levels throughout the year.

Your data can be skewed by sales and promotions, short-lived trends and advertising campaigns, so make a note of these events when they occur, and take them into consideration when making repeat stock purchases based on this data.

Average Basket Value

It may help to know the average value of your sales:

> **Basket Value =**
>
> Total Sales (£) ÷ Number of Sales

If the average sale is £27, ask yourself what you could do to raise this to £30 or even £35. Maybe you could offer free delivery or a gift when customers spend over this amount, or try cross-selling and up-selling more. The average basket value can be compared over time to check that it is not decreasing, which can be indicative of one of a number of issues, including problems with your pricing, marketing, or product variety.

How to Manage Your Stock

Stock Keeping Balance Sheet

A simple method to manage your stock is to keep a tally of all the purchases of each product, deduct its sales and 'shrinkage' (defective or stolen items), and restock any returns, as in the example below:

Figure 9.7 Stock Inventory Record

	Total Purchases	Total Sales	Total Shrinkage	Total Returns	Current Stock
Product A	150	89	0	7	68
Product B	60	10	1	0	49

If you are working with Microsoft Excel or similar spreadsheet software, you can insert a link from a running total from the total individual product sales record (see figure 9.6) to the total sales cell. The worksheet will then automatically update itself and provide you with up-to-the-minute stock information.

Current Stock Value

Having too much money tied up in stock can cause cash flow problems, so it is beneficial to keep an up-to-date record, as in Figure 9.8. Having a high amount of stock of one product is not necessarily a problem if you are turning over the stock quickly. But if items have been sitting on your shelves for a while, it might be time to clear them to make room for products that will convert into profit more quickly.

Figure 9.8 Stock Value Record

	Unit Price	Stock Quantity	Total Value
Product A	£4.34	12	£52.08
Product B	£0.52	26	£13.52
		Total Stock =	**£65.60**

The total of your current stock is a useful figure to have when taking out an insurance policy, or if you are intending to sell the business.

Contribution margin of products

Calculating the profit contribution of each single SKU, product line or range will tell you which products you should be focusing on (because they are contributing the most profit,) and which products you should discontinue, or at least investigate further (because they are performing poorly.)

Figure 9.9 Product Contribution Margin

	Gross Profit £	Units Sold	£ Product Contribution	% Profit Contribution
Product A	£6.65	60	£399.00	53.99 %
Product B	£2.80	100	£280.00	37.89 %
Product C	£4.00	15	£60.00	8.12 %
	Total Gross Profit		**£739.00**	**≈ 100 %**

To work out the contribution margins of products, you should make the following calculations:

1. Your Selling Price – Cost of Goods Sold = Gross Profit (£)
2. Gross Profit x Number of Units Sold = Product Contribution (£)
3. Product's Contribution (£) ÷ Total Gross Profit
4. x100 = Product Contribution (%)

Example:

Product A costs the retailer £4.34 and has a selling price of £10.99

1. £10.99 - £4.34 = £6.65
2. £6.65 x 60 = £399.00
3. £399.00 ÷ £739.00 = 0.5399
4. 0.5399 x 100 = 53.99%

In Figure 9.9, Products A and B are contributing most of the revenue while Product C is seriously under-performing. There could be a number of reasons for this, and the solution could be as simple as increasing the promotion of Product C, changing its price or finding an alternative brand that resonates better with customers.

Presenting the Data

In each of the examples above, just two or three records have been filled in. In real life, you may have hundreds or thousands of records, making it much harder and very time consuming to spot the patterns and irregularities from the raw data alone.

To accurately analyse and compare a lot of information, it needs to be presented in a user-friendly format. Some bookkeeping programs such as Sage automatically produce reports and charts. Spreadsheet software such as Microsoft Excel can do the job just as well, although some of the formulas may take a bit of work to get right if you are unfamiliar with them. Once your data has been converted into graphs and pie charts you'll get a clearer view of the financial workings of the business and be able to make more accurate decisions.

Making Improvements & Troubleshooting

All too often management accounting is performed by small businesses when things aren't going well. In contrast, savvy business owners continuously check performance indicators to give themselves advance warning of any problems before they become irreversible.

While all businesses encounter financial aches and pains occasionally, (such as failing to meet profit targets or struggling to pay creditors on time), these 'symptoms' are caused by one or more of three main problem areas; low incomings; high expenses; and poor cash flow management. If ignored, they can have a detrimental effect on your business's financial health. Fortunately, whatever the cause, there are plenty of possible remedies for each.

Your Incomings are Too Low

A low gross profit or even just the feeling that your sales weren't as good as expected, are signs that you need to look at improving your incomings. Typically, it can take a few years before a new business starts generating the sort of profit that makes all the hard work worthwhile, so don't be overly concerned if you have just started up.

Remedies include:

- Adjusting your selling prices to achieve optimum revenue.
- Selling more by cross-selling, up-selling, and increasing the average basket value.
- Discontinuing poor performing products that have low profit margins and low sales volumes.
- Focusing on the sales channels that bring in the most income.
- Increasing your customer base with advertising and promotions.
- Making your products more attractive with free delivery, free gifts, etc.

- Negotiating a lower unit price from your supplier, taking advantage of discounts, finding a different supplier or an alternative product in order to pass the savings onto customers and encourage sales.
- Diversifying into new markets with new products or target markets.
- Identifying and focusing on your most profitable customers.

Your Expenses are Too High

Having out-of-control expenses is a common problem, which is easy to spot if there is a considerable difference between your incomings and the profit you are left with after you've calculated your outgoings.

Remedies include:

- Performing an expenses review (see below).
- Negotiating cheaper prices with landlords and suppliers.
- Leasing equipment rather than purchasing or buying second hand.
- Finding cheaper substitutes (e.g., would a flyer work just as well as a more expensive booklet?)
- Calculating the ROI (return on investment, see below) for the sales channels with the highest outgoings.
- Reducing wastage and utilities.
- Reducing energy usage and upgrading to more efficient equipment.
- Focusing less on poorer performing customers that drain your resources.
- Joining forces with another business to share advertising, event stands, premises, etc.

Perform an Expenses Review

An expenses review is a way of identifying the costs that can be reduced, removed or put on a temporary hold, in order to save the business money in both the short and long term.

First, you should list all of your expenses in order from the biggest to the smallest. For each expense, starting with the biggest where potentially the most savings can be made, ask yourself the following questions:

- Is it essential to my operation?
- Is it providing a high enough ROI (see below)?
- Are there any cheaper alternatives available?
- What will be the consequence of eliminating this expense in the short and long term? (Will it affect quality, brand image, or customer awareness?)

Sometimes the solution can be as simple as identifying the non-essential purchases and reducing or postponing them until your business has grown some more. In other cases, it may not be cost-effective to try to lower an expense. For example, you may be able to reduce your rent and rates by relocating, but the process of moving would increase your short-term outgoings and possibly have other negative implications.

Return On Investment

Spending a large amount of money on a purchase isn't necessarily a bad thing as long as you get a good return on your investment (ROI.)
To measure whether an expense is generating a good ROI you should calculate the following:

ROI =

(Gain from Investment − Cost of Investment) - Cost of Investment

ROI as a percentage =

ROI x100

The calculation will help you decide if an expense will generate a high enough income to help you reach your profit targets. The higher the percentage the better.

You Have Cash Flow Problems

If you don't have enough money to pay your bills on time, then your business has cash flow problems. If this situation continues for any length of time, then it could actually increase your expenses. Suppliers could start charging you statutory interest, or you may need to take out a loan or overdraft and pay fees and interest. It is easy to understand how problems can spiral if business owners don't face them in time.

- Remedies include:
- Reducing the amount of money you have tied up in stock.
- Increasing your stock turnover by increasing customers and sales to release cash from stock.
- Making sure your debtors pay you on time by making your payment terms clear in your conditions. If they fail to pay on time, take immediate action.
- Reducing the period of credit you give your customers.
- Taking full advantage of any credit that suppliers offer you. If you don't have to pay immediately, then don't.
- Selling off assets (such as surplus equipment) to release cash quickly.
- Increasing your overdraft or taking out a loan.
- Increasing your prices.
- Finding an investor or investing money of your own to improve the situation.

Note that none of the remedies for the above problem areas recommend slashing prices, which is often the first thing that business owners consider doing when they encounter financial problems. It is a hasty reaction, which should always be a last resort unless you are specifically trying to capture market share or are involved in an unavoidable price war.

In the final chapter, we will look at how to plan for the future and realise your long-term vision for your jewellery and accessories business.

Thinking about the Future

In the early days of starting a new venture, when you are putting in long hours and juggling multiple roles, it can be hard to think far ahead into the future. Eventually though, as your business starts to become more established, you can let go of the reins a little and reap some of the rewards. There are not just financial benefits to running a stable enterprise, but also increased leisure time and flexibility if you want it.

Your responsibilities as an owner should evolve over time. You'll find that you spend less time firefighting and more time driving the company forward. You will need to plan long-term strategies and set challenging yet achievable objectives, to turn your dream of running a *successful* jewellery and accessories business into a reality. By understanding the strengths and weaknesses of your company, as well as the opportunities and threats that it faces, you will be able to set goals that steer your business in the right direction.

SWOT Analysis

You'll need to work out the best way to grow and improve your business in the long-term. It helps if you gain a full understanding of the internal and external situation, by analysing your Strengths, Weaknesses, Opportunities, and Threats (SWOT).

Strengths / Weaknesses

Strengths are internal factors that you perform well. They include your assets, resources, specialties, and other factors that provide you with a competitive advantage. In contrast, weaknesses are internal aspects of your business that need to be improved because either your competitors perform them better, or they are hindering your ability to meet targets. These internal factors may include:

- Brand and reputation
- Marketing strategy
- Staff
- Customer service
- Competitiveness
- Location
- Relationships with suppliers
- Equipment and technology
- Pricing
- Customer base
- Market share
- Online presence
- Products and services
- Financial position
- Stock management

Opportunities / Threats

Opportunities are external factors that can be leveraged to improve your business and help you meet targets. Threats are external factors that are out of your control, but could potentially damage your business in some way. Some of the factors listed below may not appear to be both an opportunity and a threat, but consider the consequences of not being able to take an opportunity (due to a lack of resources, for example.) If a competitor was to get a grant or your customers adopted new technology, and your business did not, it could threaten your position in the market. Other factors such as exchange rates can go up and down, and therefore be a threat or an opportunity depending on whether they are favourable to you. External factors may include:

- Available grants
- New technology
- Diversification
- Online presence
- Financial position
- Joint ventures
- Acquisitions
- Social changes
- Competitor's activities
- Competitor's pricing
- Exchange rate changes
- Interest rate changes
- Taxation changes
- Exporting to new markets
- Market growth/ decline
- Legal changes

The SWOT Analysis Matrix

To get a clear perspective on the strengths, weaknesses, opportunities and threats that are facing your business you can complete a SWOT analysis matrix. See Figure 10.1.

Once you have completed your own SWOT analysis, you should have a better idea of your capabilities and limitations, as well as the potential for future growth and improvement. You can then develop a long-term plan for your business.

Figure 10.1 Example of a completed SWOT analysis matrix

STRENGTHS	WEAKNESSES
• Good relationships with suppliers • Equipment and technology is up-to-date • Good stock inventory • Excellent location	• Staff have limited experience and skills • Low customer service rating • Local brand awareness is poor
OPPORTUNITIES	THREATS
• Grants are available • Online presence could be increased • New technology could be adopted • Taxation changes	• Competitor's attempts to take our share of the market • Interest rate increases could affect outgoings and customer spending

The Strategic Plan

The term *strategic planning* might sound as though it belongs inside a corporate boardroom, but it is just another way of describing the process of developing the long-term plans that will help turn your vision into a reality. The strategic plan doesn't have to be a lengthy document; in fact most small businesses could probably get away with writing two to three pages.

To help you formulate your strategic plan you should ask yourself the following three questions:

1. Where are we now? What is your monthly and annual turnover and profit? What percentage of market share do you possess? How satisfied are your customers? What is the public perception of your business and their level of brand awareness? How competitive are you? Are you achieving your current goals and objectives with ease or difficulty? What are your strengths and weaknesses?

2. Where do we want to be? Where do you see your business in three, five, and ten years' time? What are your long-term goals? What is the business vision and mission? What is the best way to expand and improve? What opportunities exist?

3. How are you going to get there? What resources and skills do you need? What do the individual business functions such as marketing need to do to achieve the overall objectives? What operational processes need to be improved? What attitudes need to change? Where do you need to focus your efforts in the future?

Dream Big

Deciding where you want to be in the future, what is achievable and what is unrealistic, requires objectivity. When formulating a strategic plan, some entrepreneurs are reluctant to aim high for fear of disappointment, while others have extremely high expectations of themselves and of their business. Too much pressure can be demotivating, but if you aim below your capabilities then you will eventually become dissatisfied anyway.

It is better to reach high, by choosing goals that are challenging yet achievable, even though a successful outcome is not guaranteed. When you dream big, it is unlikely that you will achieve everything that you set out to do, but you will probably be running a much more successful, personally fulfilling jewellery and accessories business.

Often, it is a good idea to ask yourself a fourth question when developing your strategic plan; where will we end up if we continue in the same direction? The answer to this is usually enough to motivate bigger ideas. After all, a business needs to grow just to maintain its current position in the market. Standing still is not an option in the jewellery and accessories industry.

You must consider the implications of future growth and improvement in your strategic plan. Your main objective could be to target new markets, which would require bigger premises and more resources such as additional staff. How you will finance and obtain these extra resources is something that you should include in the strategic plan. In other words, these are the smaller sub-steps you have to take in order to reach your ultimate goal. Therefore, try to view the 'practicalities' as challenges that you can overcome with good planning and positivity, rather than obstacles that will prevent you from achieving your big ideas.

Setting Smart Objectives

By setting targets, you can regularly assess your performance and measure how much closer you are to your vision. You'll improve your chances of success if your targets are SMART:

Specific – targets should describe exactly what you want to achieve, e.g., 'to increase market share', 'launch an online store', 'increase turnover', 'raise brand awareness'.

Measurable – measurements such as '£10,000', '12%', and '50 units', will provide a means to measure your performance.

Attainable – targets should be challenging yet attainable and you should know exactly what you need to do to achieve them.

Relevant – your goals need to support the mission and overall vision of your business, and should be worthwhile.

Timely – setting a completion date such as 'by 2025', 'in eight months,' or 'by 31st July' will improve your success rate.

An example of a smart target could be 'to increase sales turnover by 26% within 4 years.'

Monitoring Your Performance

Regularly reviewing your strategic plan and evaluating your performance will keep you focused on driving the business forward. Some companies do this on a quarterly or biannual basis, others more often. The right frequency for your business depends on the size and timescale of the tasks ahead.

These strategic performance reviews are a chance to assess the progress that has already been made, to identify what is still left to do, and to remind everyone of the goals they are working towards. Whenever you achieve or set objectives, or new opportunities or threats arise, you should make amendments to the strategic plan.

Transforming Your Role

Depending on your personal aims, your role within the business is likely to evolve over time. If your sole interest in setting up a jewellery and accessories business is in the enjoyment you get from your hobby, then your role is unlikely change much. However, if you intend to expand your business, then at some point you may need to take on staff.

Often when people first launch a business they do everything themselves: accounting, marketing, customer service, IT, picking and packing orders… Sixteen-hour days are certainly not uncommon in the beginning. There may come a time though, when your business is stable, when you'd like to focus more on the future and less on the menial day-to-day tasks.

Becoming a manager and giving other people responsibility for daily tasks can be daunting, not least because you are putting your 'baby' in the hands of others. It is, however, a great way to free up your time so that you can concentrate on growing your business.

Managing people isn't rocket science, but it is a profession. A bad manager can have a detrimental impact on an entire business because it eventually filters down to the customers. If you have little or no experience of managing people, then it might be worth considering doing a management training course, as well as researching modern leadership techniques and workplace psychology.

If you decide to hire someone to run your business for you, make sure they are qualified and have a proven track record in management. Ideally, they should also have experience in retailing jewellery and accessories.

In 'The Four-Hour Workweek', author Timothy Ferriss explains how outsourcing is another way to free up your time and achieve freedom from the tasks that you dislike. He recommends hiring a specialist company that provides remote assistants to businesses. These assistants can perform tasks such as answering emails and telephone calls, fulfilling orders, bookkeeping, social networking, search engine optimisation, etc. Incidentally, outsourcing can be an excellent way to plug an internal skills shortage, which you may have identified from your SWOT analysis.

A Final Thought

All the talk in the media of the after-effects of the recession can be worrying to owners and off-putting to those considering starting up their own business. However, many of the companies that fell victim to the recession were most likely coasting along with underlying problems long before disaster struck. Perhaps they were not keeping a close eye on their finances, or were relying heavily on a supplier that had also started sinking. Perhaps they were stuck 'doing it the way it has always been done', missing opportunities and not embracing emerging sales channels. Perhaps they simply forgot that jewellery and accessory customers value style and quality above all else. Whatever the reason(s), we only have to look to the ones that survived, and are thriving, in this still-precarious economic climate to know that the recession alone was not to blame for businesses failing.

Succeeding in this sector requires flexibility, forward thinking and a constant juggling of all of the activities discussed in this book. Most of all, it requires a passion for jewellery and accessories.

References

Ariely, D. 2008. *Predictably Irrational: The Hidden Forces that Shape our Decisions.* Harper Collins.

Baines, P., Fill, C., and Page, K. 2010. *Marketing, Second Edition.* Oxford: OUP.

Ferriss, T. 2009. The Four-Hour Workweek: Escape 9-5, Live Anywhere, and Join The New Rich. New York: Crown.

Godin, S. 1999. Permission Marketing: Turning Strangers into Friends and Friends into Customers. New York: Simon & Schuster.

Middleston, S. 2010. *Build a Brand in 30 Days: With Simon Middleton, The Brand Strategy Guru.* Chichester: Capstone.

Nagle, T., Hogan, J. and Zale, J. 2010. *The Strategy and Tactics of Pricing, 5th Edition.* Prentice Hall.

Weetman, P. 2010. *Management Accounting, Second Edition.* Financial Times/ Prentice Hall.

Websites
www.businesslink.gov.uk
www.cipd.co.uk
www.designcouncil.org.uk
www.elmsbury.com
www.inc.com

Resources

Suppliers and B2B Directories

www.alibaba.com
www.aliexpress.com
www.amber-jewellery.com
www.globalsources.com
www.westerncounties.co.uk
www.smallvolume.com
www.thewholesaler.co.uk

Marketing and Networking

https://twitter.com
www.bttradespace.com
www.constantcontact.com
www.facebook.com
www.google.co.uk/adwords
www.mailchimp.com
www.surveymonkey.com
www.linkedin.com

Shows and Trade Events

www.asiafja.com
www.ifjag.com
www.bijorhca.com
www.enkshows.com
www.moda-uk.co.uk
www.springfair.com
www.autumnfair.com
www.thejewelleryshowlondon.com

Trade Publications

www.accessoriesmagazine.com
www.attiremagazines.com
www.jewelleryfocus.co.uk
www.thejewellermagazine.com
www.retail-jeweller.com
www.professionaljeweller.com

General Business Information

www.britishchambers.org.uk
www.companieshouse.gov.uk
www.gov.uk/browse/business
www.hmrc.gov.uk

Ecommerce, Website and Mobile Site Providers

www.ekmpowershop.com
www.jimdo.com
www.lemonstand.com
www.magentocommerce.com
www.mymcart.com
www.oscommerce.com
www.prestashop.com
www.shopify.com
www.weebly.com
www.wordpress.org
www.wordpress.com
www.zen-cart.com

Index